Praise for Silencing Fear

"I have had the honor and privilege of being Tina's pastor for many years. I have witnessed, first hand, every word of this book fleshed out throughout her life.

I know this God inspired book will be used to silence the liar, fear, and to lead so many people into the beautiful freedom God has promised you and I, as His sons and daughters.

If you are ready to walk free from torment and free from fear this is your book!"

~Bené Marsh
Pastor, Epic Church
Decatur, AL

"Tina is precious! We absolutely adore her heart and passion for Jesus and others! We feel privileged to be a small part in her journey of knowing God and having a relationship with Him. *Silencing Fear* is a raw, true story so that others can be encouraged, find Jesus and freedom from fear."

~Charley and Shari Cain
Pastors, World Harvest Outreach
Hartselle, AL

"I am so thankful that my beautiful friend, Tina Sims, stepped out in obedience to share her story in her book, *Silencing Fear*. This is not an easy subject to talk about, especially in the church. However, it is a subject that we have all experienced and struggled with at some point in our lives. When Tina first came to me and asked me to pray about writing this book, I knew there was already something prophetic and powerful on her story. She has lived the words she has penned on these pages, and she has overcome the FEAR that has tried to take her captive.

She confronts fear and has learned to defeat it through the Word and prayer. If you deal with fear or know someone who does, this book will navigate you/them back to HIS word and heart."

~Kim Aube
Pastor, The Rock Family Worship Center
Madison, AL

"When you lie down, you will not be afraid;
when you lie down, your sleep will be sweet."

Proverbs 3:24

Silencing Fear

By Tina C. Sims

Journey into God's Overcoming Power

Silencing Fear

Copyrighted 2019 by Tina C. Sims

Author Photo: *Ally Patterson*
Cover Artist: *Melissa Hopper*
Cover Design: *Kristie LaRochelle/kpstudios.com*

Unless otherwise indicated, all Scripture quotations are from the Holy Bible, New International Version, copyright 2018, by Tyndale House Foundation.

ISBN: 9781077935679

Other Books by this author:

"As the Sun Rises"
Encouragement for Your Day

Dedication

I dedicate this book to my prayer circle. Thank you-April Hitt, Christy Bunch, Diane Valencia, Kim Thurston, Laura Murphy, Lori Marks and Tina Reeves. Each of you are so special to me and this book. I love you all, and I love the friendship we have! Your prayers and encouragement saw this through to the finish line.

Acknowledgments

To my husband Tommy-thank you for your endless love and support. In Everything. Always.

Mom and Dad-thank you for reading my first draft start to finish the minute I sent it to you. That alone speaks your love.

My niece Ally-thank you for your encouragement for a finished product and a vision to write.

Jessica Jetton-thank you for our conversations as God has grown both of us. You are a gift!

Beth Schoenberger-thank you for your constant enthusiasm and willingness to help in any way.

Lori Marks-thank you for your time editing-it was the perfect help at the perfect time.

Pastor IV and Bene' Marsh-your love and encouragement are in all you do. Thank you.

Connie Teague-thank you for being my personal prayer warrior when I was writing the most. Your prayers kept my thoughts going!

Pastor Charley and Shari Cain, Pastor CB Durbin, Pastor Kim Aube, Starla Such, Michelle Patterson and Marie Griffin-thank you for reading that first draft-your comments of encouragement-gave me courage to continue!

Keith Carrol, my Literary Agent-You are a light. Thank you for your taking me on as a client and leading me through this journey of completion.

Anna Hurst-thank you for your guidance and help with editing! Your red marks of correction are making me better and better!

God-you walk with me and talk with me. Thank you that I am one of your own and that your story is still being written within me.

Table of Contents

Introduction

When I sat down to write my acknowledgements (the final step for me finishing this book), I remembered a dream I had approximately three years ago. My husband, Tommy, and I were strolling through an old flea market. My teenage niece, Ally, was with us on our shopping journey and was following us at a distance. Hallways and doors into more booths ahead of us with each step; dark and dusty with all kinds of great old things to look at.

We walked along and repeatedly a large man with impressive muscles and outstanding height stepped out into our path.

The man had his arms crossed and his feet firmly planted each time. His intent was to block us, perhaps harm us but to certainly not let us continue. Yet, each time we got close to him he would step into the darkness and out of our way. And each time I would look back at my niece.

Then, Tommy and I would walk past the man.

At the time of the dream, I had a conversation with a friend of mine about it, Pastor Bené Marsh and I discussed the flea market being something old and representing my past.

We discussed the man wanting to block my way to what was next, continually stepping out in front of me. Satan. The one who could not keep me from going where I wanted to go next, but that he certainly wanted me to think he could. We discussed who was with me. Beside me, my husband, Tommy. Behind me, my niece, Ally.

Now, I realize that dream was about this book. "Surrendering Fear." My biggest desire was to keep it simple. To revisit my past and have my teenage niece and someone like my long-ago teenage self-understand and follow along. And Tommy walking with me as well.

I have struggled with fear within my dreams and fear in and of the dark off and on my entire life. The struggle is over; I am now free, free to share and free to help others grow, even as I am still growing.

God is bigger and wants to help you and strengthen you to overcome also!

Life is such an incredible journey!

Full of stories, our stories. Stories that God gives each of us to share with others, for us all to become closer to Him, to know Him more and to overcome Satan's attacks in our lives.

This part of my "story" is what God has grown in my heart while learning to trust God and walk in his authority. A journey of dreams, visions and encounters from the dark side of life, but ESPECIALLY my learning about God's all conquering power that lives within God's people!

This includes me and you!

**"God IS our refuge and our strength,
an
ever-present
help
in
trouble"
(Psalm 46:1).**

It took me quite a while to get to this place of freedom. But, but, but the story of getting there is complete. It is a wonderful place to understand who you are and whose you are.

From the moment we are born, God has a plan for each of us. How much we seek Him is up to us. But in the seeking is where we find freedom. Freedom from whatever has kept us bound.

Freedom into all that God has for each of us!

Thank you for spending your time reading. I am praying and trusting for God to reveal His complete overcoming power in your own life as you do!

Tina C. Sims

1- "Fear Enters"

My childhood bedroom was small and cozy with a twin bed. Look inside and you would have found a beautiful handmade "Dutch Dolls" quilt, a Barbie or two, a few books and my favorite stuffed animal. Everything a little girl needed.

A huge window gave me the sunshine and the moon, always filling my room with light. Above my bed, to the right of where I slept was that big single window. Perfectly, it was positioned up high on the wall, higher than my height. This made it easy to look up and out at the night sky as I lay in bed. I loved to do that. Lying comfy in my bed, I would wonder about the rest of the world as I counted the stars, searching and searching for one to fall so I could make a wish. This was my personal space and I loved it. As the stars twinkled and the moon glowed, I was content.

This bedroom was not a scary place for me. I was not a fear- filled child. Meaning, I did grow up having or wanting a night light. The dark itself did not scare me. I was the first to want to play the game "hide go seek" outside at night and often I would hide in a dark closet forever waiting on someone to find me. I would've thought I was normal. I laugh at this now. What is normal anyway? None of us are normal. God has big things for all of us, and Satan will try hard to stop us even starting at young age!

Indeed, he did try.

Vividly, I can still remember myself in that small bed enjoying my bedtime and bedroom. But just as vividly, I can remember when I became paralyzed with fear for the very first time; it was also there in the private, personal space of my little room.

Now, when I said paralyzed, I really do mean paralyzed. I was unable to turn my head, not even a smidgen. My little legs, my skinny arms, my fingers and my toes were as if they had disappeared. I could not budge. The feeling of a heavy weight on top of me had me unable to move. I opened my mouth to scream but nothing came out. As my heart beat picked up and the tears started to flow, the terror grew stronger!

With good reason!

Something was in my room, and it was right beside my bed!

Out of the corner of my eye, I could see something dark close to the left side of my face! My mouth wide open, I tried again and again-to scream for my parents to come help me! But no voice of mine could be found! I wanted to get up and run, but I couldn't! My body failed to cooperate!

I tightly squeezed my eyes shut, but I could still feel the meanness of what was beside me! I was so scared! Terrified, I lay trembling in fear.

Peeking my eyes open, I could see a dark form beside me. What was it? Where did it come from? Was it going to kill me? My breathing became difficult like I was suffocating, and I felt as if I was being pushed further and further down on my bed.

I search even now for words to describe what I saw.

Let's imagine you are outside and you have your shadow following you as you walk. Well, now imagine that shadow walking into a room that you are already in, all by itself. Go ahead and imagine it is not your shadow but someone else's, and even that does not seem frightening enough.

Imagine a mass of darkness, having no eyes, no nose, lips, or other facial features, a shape blocking the light, a darkness within the dark, one that is capable of moving around. This is what I saw. Right beside me as I lay in bed!

Now, imagine it wanted to kill you. This is what I felt!

Then, the darkness spoke! A deep masculine voice, barely above a whisper said to me, "Where were we?" My brain did not register an answer to this question, not that I could have answered anyway. I was too afraid to speak or think. But again, I heard, "Where were we?"

I have pondered this question for many years because this visit, this exact visit, happened over and over again. Always the same question, always the same position of the darkness by my head. Always the same paralyzing and immobilizing fear. The air in my room always seemed thick; I could feel the hatefulness. Fear and hate filled the room up like smoke from a fire.

I think the answer to the "Where were we?" question that it asked about was the pits of hell! That is surely what it felt like! Can you even picture this? Can you imagine a seven-year-old child being tormented in this way? I was every word that has ever been spoken about being afraid.

Many instances of the dark shadow sliding into my room occurred, and sometimes it didn't speak. I wished I could tell you this made it less scary. But no, creeping in, like how fog rolls into the forest, I could feel the horrible overwhelming heaviness as it moved into my bedroom.

It was there to frighten me, to make me believe it had power over me, to show itself as evil and to make me fear for my life and bodily harm. And, it worked! I was one scared little girl.

I came to hate my bedroom, and I hated to lie down at night. Fear of something being on top of me pushing the life out of me filled me all the time. Surely, whatever it was, was going to kill me.

I did not understand any of this. I became fearful of every noise when it was dark. I checked my closet; I checked under my bed. Then, I would check again.

I became scared of the dark itself. Being outside at night was no longer fun. I was even scared of what I would see out of my window, so I stopped looking out. Coming home from my friends next door became a high-speed run if it was no longer daylight. Some days I even avoided visiting the neighbors and playing outside if it was close to getting dark.

Yet, the "visits" continued. I am not sure how long these visits lasted. Hours? Minutes that seemed like hours? Oh, how I wanted this to stop. How I hoped it would go away, and when it was present, how I wished I could call out for help and oh, how I now wished for a nightlight!

But when the evil presence or what I perceived as a ghost was gone, it was gone and so was I! The very moment that I could move, I did. With the speed of an Olympic Sprinter, I would run to my parents' room, seeking protection and consoling.

Mom let me in bed with them for the first few times. I would nudge her awake. As I shook and sniffled, I would tell her I had something scary in my room. She would pull back the covers, and I would quickly snuggle in, quiet not to wake my Dad.

It seemed that my behavior got old pretty quick. Three people in one bed, I suppose they were not fans.

So, I was "encouraged" to stay in bed. I think they thought I was making it all up just to get to snuggle. Not a bad idea but not what was happening either.

Next, I found refuge in my brother's room. But my parents were not happy with me when they found me there either, and then my brother started getting in trouble for not sending me back to my room.

The situation did help me get smarter. I created a strategy. I began to wait until everyone was asleep, grab my little "Doll-Girl" quilt, sneak into my brother's room, lay down in the floor beside his bed and sleep. Then, I would tiptoe out before anyone got up.

And it worked!

Not being by myself prevented the doom I found in my own bedroom alone. Nothing came in and bothered me when I was with someone else. We could start a new conversation right here, couldn't we? All bad stuff seems worse if we are alone, and some bad stuff really will leave if we are not left alone with it and get help... But...

What was THIS in my room? The Boogeyman? People were always making jokes about The Boogeyman. "Be good, or The Boogeyman will get you," people would say. "Had I not been good?" I wondered. I did not think that I had been bad or disobedient when these night visits happened. So, I decided it was not the Boogeyman.

Was this a ghost? Because I knew about ghosts! Just not bad ones who scared little kids!

"The Alabama Ghosts" and others like it were a daily part of my second-grade classroom at this time. "Story time," we called it, was one of the best parts of my school day. We kids would gather around our teacher as she sat in a chair and read.

Ghost stories had become my favorite. Several stories had been read; we had several left to read, and I believed every word.

There was a story of man who had been hanged, who was very tall. The hangman had to dig a hole under the man's feet for him to die by the noose because the tree limb was not tall enough to get the man's feet off of the ground so the man would die. The story told us that a ghost kept the hole swept out daily, never letting leaves stay in it.

I still remember another story of a man's face being imprinted on a window after he was struck by lightning while looking out of it. People would replace the pane of glass, and the face would always return.

That was a lot of spooky stuff, probably too much information for a lot seven-year-olds. Looking back, it's pretty obvious it was too much for me.

Ghosts? The books my teacher read had pictures in them. I was one of those kids who sat close and soaked in any kind of story, and these were no different. None of the stories she read had anything about mean ghosts who came after people. Most of them we read about looked all pretty and white, floating around like a cloud.

I remember thinking about the ghosts a lot. I remember looking for them in my grandmother's home and her neighbors' because it was older. Being curious, I asked people if anyone had died in their house. I probably wanted to see one of the pretty lady ghosts with a big flowing gown like in one of the books.

I certainly would never have wanted to see what I saw!

During some of my "nightmare incidents," my Mom went to my school and had a meeting with my teacher. My claims of having a ghost being in my room had gotten me in all kinds of trouble at home. (I wasn't *always* clever enough to not get caught changing rooms at night.)

My Mom had my teacher remove me from the classroom during story time until the series of ghost stories was finished. The school library had some of these books, and I had been checking them out to bring home to read. That also got stopped.

I remember being upset about this. I liked the ghost stories, and I certainly didn't like having to sit out in the hall during story time, it was embarrassing. I was made fun of and even called names. But I now believe with all my heart this was a wise decision that my parents made for me.

But sitting out in the hall turned out to be Okay. My friend, Tressie, would sit out in the hall with me and keep me company. She wasn't having any "nightmares," so I guess we just talked and giggled about second grade stuff.

We are still friends to this day. This is great picture of God being ahead of us, removing me from a situation not good for me and sending someone along to help. Thank you, Tressie Mullins, for being my friend and choosing to hang out with me in the hall. You have always been awesome!

I am sure my parents were praying. Maybe even my teacher who had to put me in that hall. Perhaps, Jesus himself. (The Bible does tell us Jesus prays for us to The Father.) I was learning to pray, and I was praying, praying for the darkness to never come back.

Some "things" did shift after I was removed from the ghost stories. This is also when I begin to understand they could be bad, that they could be helping frighten me.

God had a plan then, and He has one now. His plan is for His kids, big and little, for all of us, to know Him personally. For each of us to know what The Bible says and the power in what it says, for each of us to live in that and to understand it for ourselves.

Sitting in my bedroom before bed one night, I got my Bible out to look at the pictures but instead stopped and read the inside cover. There I found the 23rd Psalm written with pretty red letters, which quickly became a favorite. That Children's Bible is still a favorite too; thankfully, I still have it.

It is a small one that has a picture of Jesus with children all around him on the front cover. Jesus is on a donkey (in color) and everyone is wearing robes and head dresses, a beautiful scene of Jesus riding into Bethlehem. Open it and on the inside of the front cover it has the 23rd

Psalm and an "I love you from Mommy and Daddy" note from when I was four-years-old.

My Bible was the King James Revised Version. King James did not make a lot of sense to me. Nor did I know or care who King James was. But the inside cover, that psalm was about not being afraid, and boy, did I know about that, so I memorized the entire thing even with its "thees and thous!" A scared, motivated kid can do this in like two days!

I knew what being afraid was, and I did not want to be afraid anymore. I wanted the "fear no evil" part of what Psalm 23 said! I still can recite this Psalm. It will forever remain one of my favorite scriptures.

While I now prefer the NIV version, the Psalm was printed in my childhood Bible like this:

Psalm 23

The Lord is my shepherd,
I shall not want;
He makes me lie down in green pastures.
He leads me beside still waters;
He restores my soul.
He leads me in paths of righteousness
for his name's sake.

Even though I walk through the
valley of the shadow of death,
I fear no evil;
for thou art with me;
thy rod and thy staff,
they comfort me.

Thou preparest a table before me
in the presence of my enemies;
thou anointest my head with oil,
my cup overflows.

Surely goodness and mercy shall follow me
all the days of my life;
and I shall dwell in the house of the Lord
forever.

Verse four, "Even though I walk through
the valley of the shadow of death, I fear
no evil, for thou art with me; thy rod
and thy staff they comfort me," and verse
six "Surely goodness and mercy shall
follow me all the days of my life; and I

. the house of the Lord
ə the ones I loved the most.

Forever.

ı⌐ would fear no evil. Forever,
goodnes⌐ and mercy would follow me.
Forever, I would dwell in God's house, a
safe place, forever.

At the time, I did not comprehend the
true power of learning The Bible, these
words, these promises. But the darkness
that was coming to me at night did. I
believed Psalm 23, I was more peaceful, I
felt less afraid. I began to believe that
God could protect me and would continue
to protect me!

I would repeat Psalm 23 from start to
finish out loud, over and over again
while lying in my bed. I stopped sneaking
into my brother's room to sleep as often.
I started sleeping better in my own room
and checking out the stars through my
window again. I would look out my bedroom
window into the night sky and recite "my"
psalm over and over. My heart and room
were full of peace.

When I would say, "I fear no evil," I
found a courage, I had not had. Repeating
the Psalm increased my courage and
nothing was coming to me at night! I was
gaining ground; God was helping me!

I doubt very seriously I understood much else about the Psalm. I am sure I didn't know what a rod or a staff was. I did like green pastures and streams of water, but I did not have a clue about anointing oil or what to do with it until I was much older. And as for "the shadow of death," well, this presence had me thinking I was going to die from it. Maybe I was even seeing it, the shadow of death.

But! But! But! God's word IS God's word!

What I understand now is our enemy, Satan, understood God's word and had to submit to it. If I could have understood this one thing completely and continued to even just repeat that one Psalm and believe only a couple of lines, this life-long journey could have looked a lot different! That Psalm, my very first scripture memorization, had brought peace and courage where there was none.

Pause a moment and think about that!

What does God's word say about what you are going through?

LOOK it up!

Ask someone!

Get it in your heart!

Read it, write it down, and memorize it.

Then read it aloud over yourself as you
believe it for yourself!

KNOW GOD IS YOUR HELP-

"Your word is a lamp to my feet." Psalm 119:105

"Every word of God proves true; he is a shield to those who take refuge in him." Proverbs 30:5

"For God is not a God of disorder but of peace." 1 Corinthians 14:33

"The thief (Satan) comes to steal kill and destroy; I have come that they may have life and have it to the full." John 10:10

"Be sober-minded; be watchful. Your adversary the devil prowls around like a roaring lion, seeking someone to devour."

2- "Shifting Shadows"

As I became a walking recital of Psalm 23, my nighttime continued to change for the better. Sweet sleep and no more getting in trouble for getting out of bed or turning my light on. After having several months of turmoil, I received several months of relief!

Whoohoo, Yippee, Amen, and Hallelujah!

But then, but then, a new visit…

Visit? Should I call it that? Who knows what to call it? An encounter maybe? Regardless, "it" happened and was different from all the previous incidents. This memory is marked in my mind like it happened yesterday. Every detail is as if I am watching it right now on TV.

You know those little chicken-skin goose bumps? Even now, they are on my arms as I think about it.

Awakened from sleep, I heard someone calling my name from the living room. "Tina, Tina, Tina," I heard. I scooted quietly out of bed, walked down the hall and into the living room. I was not afraid; I was expecting to find my brother with his hand in a box of cereal or wanting to show me something on tv.

But there was no one there; the house was quiet, the living room dark. I turned and headed to my brother's room; certain he was messing with me as he often did. But he was in bed asleep. I returned to the living room for who knows why; maybe I wanted some of that cereal. Perhaps, I was braver than I remember.

"Tina," I again heard someone say! The voice seemed to come from outside. Then, looking out of our big window on the back of our house, in the moonlight, I saw the source of my seeker. Someone or something looking very ghost like was coming rapidly through the field towards me; faster and faster it was approaching me, calling my name.

Brilliantly lit and radiantly shining on everything it passed; it appeared to be a person made completely of light! The size and build of the radiance I saw was male. A big man. He was so large! He reminded me of the then popular TV character "The Hulk." A big man with big muscles. Large, larger than anyone I had ever seen before. The vision was tall, broad shouldered, unnaturally big and unnaturally bright!

Dumbfounded, I stood watching as it continued to get closer and closer to my house. The ground and trees were beautifully lit as what I saw walked through them, and the body of what was walking appeared to be blazing as it got closer.

I suddenly became scared! Was this the scary, shadowy figure that had been coming to my room? Oh, no! I was "outta" there! Back in sprinter mode, I ran fast to my room thinking it wouldn't come this time, thinking I could say my psalm and keep him out.

If it was "it"-I was wrong!

Soon my room was overcome with darkness. It became dark like in a cave or a room with no windows. Darkest black, PITCH BLACK. I could not see even an inch in front of me. My room was darker than it had ever been, and I was more scared than I had ever been. I was struggling to breathe. Shaking uncontrollably, I lay clutching my covers tight.

My fear had returned. I was overcome. Overwhelmed to be in this same situation, I tried again and again to scream. Nothing! I felt I was surely going to die from not being able to breathe!

I squeezed my eyes closed-tight. I shut out everything and the 23rd Psalm started working in my head. I started repeating it over and over and over. "Even though I walk through the valley of the shadow of death, I fear no evil. I fear no evil. I fear no evil. God is with me. I fear no evil. I will dwell in the house of the Lord forever. I fear no evil."

I still remember saying that over and over. *"I fear no evil." God will protect me. God will protect me."*

And God did!

Next, I felt "it" leave. Yes, leave. The change in the pressing and stiffness of my body seemed immediate; I felt the darkness leave even with my eyes shut as if I could see it waltz its shadowy self-right out my door. I did not feel like something was suffocating me and holding me down; I was free. I could move. I was not scared. I did not feel even a little afraid; I KNEW it was gone.

I opened my eyes; there was moonlight in my room again, and I still remember the air smelling clean, fresh like right after a rain.

God had won, and God smelled good too!

Knowing what God said to me through the Bible and using it against what I was fighting had won. God promises us that with him we don't have to fear evil, and me believing that really did work! Knowing that changed the experience and changed me!

But what of the glowing hulk like man? Did the man full of light come to help me? I am not certain of the answer to this one yet, but I am inclined to believe that he was not good and to think that he did not come to help and that he was not an angel from God.

In the Bible, when we see an angel show itself to a human, the angel immediately recognizes the person's fear. The first thing an angel always spoke was "do not be afraid," and then they shared why they had come.

History shows us over and over: when an angel appears, it addresses our fear and then gives the message it was sent to give.

All I received is more fear, no message, and no reassurance. Doesn't sound like the goodness of God, does it? And it does not line up with the appearance of angels. Then, in speaking promises from The Bible, what was visiting me left. I think an angel would have stuck around and celebrated with me!

I know I have some understanding left to receive on this.

BUT-

After this horrific episode was over, I got up and started moving some of my things around in my room, even throwing a few things into the hall. Within the dark I did this. Unafraid, I did this. I do not remember exactly why I threw stuff out or what I threw out. Maybe life is symbolic even as a second grader. "Out with the bad, in with the good."

I woke the house up with my "house cleaning." My brother will tell you this is the night I threw the Boogieman out and quit having nightmares.

Because it really was a game changer; never again did I go to his room seeking refuge.

I do wish I could tell you it was only a nightmare. I also wish I could tell you that this night was the end of it all, but that would not be true… But as my life changed, as my faith grew, the experiences continued to change. And indeed, I did not have any experiences with crippling fear for a very long time.

Now, do I think that there is a direct relationship to the ghost stories and the evil presence showing up in my bedroom? I believe there could be. What affects one person does not affect everyone. But God's word gives us plenty of advice on guarding our hearts and minds against such things. So, if we need that advice, then obviously there can be a connection, an opening for Satan, for evil, a door for fear to come into hearts and minds.

We are told in Philippians 4:8,

"Whatever is true, whatever is noble, whatever is right, whatever is pure, whatever is lovely, whatever is admirable, if anything is excellent or praiseworthy, think about such things."

God encourages this because the devil is described as a roaring lion (a violent creature) who is walking around looking for someone to devour (1 Peter 5:7-8). Satan was and is still looking for lives to destroy, including children's lives like mine. Satan wanted to begin a lifelong process of destroying my soul, my body, my mind and my emotions.

Let's pause here. What we have going into our minds is important. Are we reading God's word? Are we looking at the positive? Are we concentrating on our fear or what scripture says? Do we even know what scripture says about a situation? If we are going to claim any type of victory, we must start there.

We must read The Bible. We must pursue understanding it. We must do our homework.

As I have sought answers in the quest to write this book, other resources have helped me see some things very clearly. One book asked questions about involvement with the occult, the Ouija board, levitation and other such topics.

Well, even by this young age, I had a neighbor who had a Ouija board. I had a toy called a Magic Eight ball and wore it out, shaking it and asking it questions. I had even been at more than one spend the night party, where we, as young girls, called out "light as a feather and stiff as a board" to attempt to levitate. As kids, we had practiced having séances.

So, to be very clear, I had perhaps opened the door for a foul presence or two to walk in. Perhaps, I was the one who cracked the door on something demonic wanting to overtake me, and I just wasn't aware of it.

The Bible describes Satan as a sneaky fellow! Remember he was first described in The Bible in physical form as a snake. Snakes are sneaky and like to hide under stuff and in stuff! Also, in Genesis 4:7 it describes sin as sneaky too. "Sin is crouching at your door; it desires to have you, but you must master it."

Sin is anything that is not of God. In perspective, I was messing with things that were not of God and consequences had certainly been coming my way.

As I go through the memories in my mind and journals, I have looked at all good and all bad. Praying and longing for answers, I have remembered all kinds of possible contributing factors.

I remember spending a lot of time with my grandmother as a child, as much time as my parents would allow. My Mom's Mom, my "Ma-Maw" I called her; gosh, I loved her, and I still miss her. She lived by herself my entire life, and as a child, I thought she was brave in doing so.

But, looking back now, she wasn't as brave as I had thought. Fear can have us behave radically. I remember her getting the house ready for us to go to bed at night, and it was extreme.

Very extreme.

Her two exterior doors she locked with two different locks and then she placed chairs against the door knobs for even more security. Then, all the windows were checked to be certain they too were locked. When we went to bed, the bedroom where we slept together (that part you now know I loved), that door was also locked with the door knob lock and then locked with a chain lock. That's a lot of locks.

I don't remember thinking much about this then. It was just what she did. It is what I helped her with. But I see now how very afraid she was at night. Her behavior was different during the day. All windows up during the summer and the front and rear door wide open for sunlight and breezes to come through the screen doors.

Obviously, my "Ma-Maw" was quite afraid of what could go bump in the night.

As a grown up, I now see how quickly and easily a child can take on emotions of others. Especially ones they respect and love, even without realizing it.

So, do I think some of this appearance of fear in my life was from staying with my Ma-Maw at night? Do I think some of what I was going through was from seeing her "overly lock up" the house? Did I take on some of her fear? I definitely think it is possible and certainly think it is very important.

Learned behavior is real. The definition for learned behavior is: actions or reactions of a person from being taught either intentionally or unintentionally from watching another. Was I being taught to be afraid of the dark? Unintentionally? Absolutely.

We can add these things together. We have me-a sensitive kid, reading ghost stories, playing games of the occult, and being shown excessive fear of the dark or harm during the night from someone they love. And we must acknowledge that Satan wants any opportunity to destroy us all, and he will come at us in any way he can and at any age he can.

Looks like a bad blend of ingredients for a child to lie down with at night.

And what if, what if the vision or experience with the man made of light was "Hulk Like" because I had also watched that tv show. The Hulk, on the TV, was a normal man, who when angered became larger than life, green and mean looking. My imagination sure was getting a lot of help, wasn't it?

Is that all that was going on? Fear and imagination?

Not entirely, Satan is a dark force indeed, and I know I will get the answer to it all when I arrive in Heaven. What I do know is what I went through was very, very difficult. Understanding it all completely is not as important as understanding what God says about it and walking that out-meaning never going through it again.

Because this is where the change came, for the better, from a little girl slammed up scared when the sun went down every day. Chokingly afraid, paralyzingly afraid, to the point of willing to get in trouble to not be alone. Scared to go to bed every single night.

To being bolder and less fearful, latched on to a set of promises in scripture and holding on tight, and finding God's victory over the darkness.

Regardless of why I was under attack, let's look at this simply.

Let's look at how such a positive shift was made at this point.

#1-I was removed from the situation of ghost stories. This changed my physical presence.

#2-I changed my behavior. I stopped playing scary games possibly linked to the occult.

#3-I learned scripture on what I was going through-fear.

#4-I believed in what I learned.

#5-I focused on the promise in the scripture instead of the fear.

#6-The "fear" left! God was my help!

This reminds me of the words of a beautiful hymn that just overwhelms my heart now that I understand it:

"Turn your eyes upon Jesus, Look full in His wonderful face. And the things of earth will grow strangely dim. In the light of His glory and grace."

Focus, I was learning to focus, to focus on God, focus on good things.

I had learned God was bigger than this darkness that had welled up so much fear and anxiety within me. In the first book of John, John explains that God is light and that in God there is no darkness at all. It even says, "at all." I didn't quite understand that yet, nor did I understand how to walk with that light and in that light, but this story is not over yet either.

Isaiah 26:3 points us in this direction even more:

"You will keep in perfect peace those whose minds are steadfast, because they trust in you."

Steadfast is defined as being resolute, focused and dutifully firm and unwavering.

And...I still needed to learn to be steadfast.

Because regardless of what I had learned, regardless of my part in it or not-my experiences were real. Something real had come to me and at me. And it still wanted to defeat me.

<u>Personal Notes</u>

3- "Joining Forces"

After the memorable night where I saw the "man made of light" and threw half of my belongings out into the hall, I actually had three to four years without being bothered… Unless you count me drawing "The Hulk" on the walls of my bedroom and our hallway.

In ink. More than once.

This created a different kind of "bothering" with my Mom. New wisdom came- do not draw on the walls!

I am laughing now, but I imagine I was trying to process and understand through my "artwork." What I actually learned was how to wash the walls and help paint.

But still, no Boogeyman, no feeling of something lurking around me, inside or outside. No dark, scary presences in my bedroom-seen or unseen, no uncontrollable fear. Only peace.

Overcoming all these fearful experiences was better than good.

Here is something else that I slowly became aware of-my radar for scary stuff, it was off the charts. I had gained a higher sense of "things that make your hair stand up" through my previous experiences.

You would not find me watching a horror movie or anything remotely spooky. The commercials themselves scared me enough and made me remember my experiences. I already believed in everything evil and everything scary. I did not need any help being afraid, and I didn't want to know anything else about it!

I started getting better with leaving stuff that felt like that "dark shadow" alone. I had quit reading books about ghosts. I quit playing the games with my neighbors. I would not take part in the "séances" that my childhood friends thought were fun.

It was not because I believed the dark presence would return that I changed my behavior. I didn't understand it like that yet. It was because I was so scared of all of it! It was real!

I am thankful that God's plan was to make certain that I knew how very real He was also! I could feel His presence as I looked out my window all the time. His warmth was with me everywhere I went.

But also, there were many occasions following those first childhood experiences where I felt the presence of something bad wrong without looking for it!

Once, while staying the weekend at a friend's house around the age of eleven, fear came out of nowhere. We had been having a great time, and I paused playing for a bathroom break. As I walked by the bedroom of my friend's brother, I felt fear grip me; chills ran up my spine. I felt like I was in slow-motion all of a sudden.

I can still see the moment clearly; I was just walking past his room, walking down the hall to their bathroom and felt the terror as I went to pass his door. The pounding of my own heart in my ears was thundering loud and increasing by the moment.

His bedroom door was shut; I had not ever even looked in his room. But I could feel something on the other side of his closed door. The presence of something mean was pressing towards me through the walls, and man, I could feel it.

Fear. Was. Back.

My feet could not get me down the hall towards the living room fast enough. I ran like a wild child! Safely away from his room, calmness returned to me. I did not tell anyone. My "crazy ghost stories" had not went over well before; no one had believed me. So, I kept this to myself.

I was wiser though. I would wait and go the to the bathroom when someone else was going to that part of the house. That worked. But I could still FEEL the pressing of something hateful as I passed his doorway, even when someone was with me. Gosh, does that make sense at all?

"Was what had come to me at night on the other side of those walls?" I wondered. Looking back at this particular instance, I know he was older than us, a teenager. I don't know what he was involved in then, but if I was a gambling kind of gal, I would place all my quarters on him being involved in something that was the opposite of Jesus at that moment!

Many times after this I would feel that same darkness that I had felt in my room in another person. This was hard to understand then, not so much now as an adult. What we are involved in can attach itself to us. Kind of like putting on a coat of happiness or wearing one of darkness and despair.

I have placed my hand on the doorknob of a person's home and felt the exact same fear I had as a child. I have been in a room full of people and felt that darkness at my back.

We recognize what we have previously experienced just like we recognize food that we have previously tasted.

It really is that simple.

Over the years, I have had small conversations of what this is like. I say small because most people do not want to believe that Satan is real in a *real* type way. And they really, really don't want to talk about it. But Satan is real! He is our enemy; he is the darkness.

It is easy to see why Satan wants us to be afraid. Fear keeps each of us from all kinds of goodness that God has planned. Good things like enjoying your family, your blessings and even your sleep; perhaps, even serving the Lord. Whether it is fear of your loved ones being in a car wreck, a fear of being alone, fear of failure, fear of being abused, fear of the weather or my own fear of "what goes bump in the night."

Fear is fear!

Fear is defined as an unpleasant emotion caused by the belief that someone or something is dangerous, likely to cause pain, or a threat. I think we would all agree with that definition. Our emotions partnered with belief that something is going to cause us harm can be overwhelming.

I certainly know this to be accurate in my life. One hundred percent, throw the towel in. Unpleasant emotion seems a little light as a definition. I could define unpleasant in a very ugly way based on my memories!

Fear can come from things that have happened to us. I have had friends have their homes and lives torn apart by a tornado. They have developed a fear of tornados and the weather because of this experience. At the mention of a storm, they are full of fear. That makes sense to all of us.

Some fear we gain from pondering "what if" even when we have never experienced the situation. This unpleasant emotion is an override of our senses by letting our mind run ahead of a situation.

If we go back to that "overwhelming" part, that is where my story started. For me it was being in the middle of something that caused not just "unpleasant emotion" but also removed my ability to react.

"Crippling." Meaning we can't move forward.

I want to ask you to think about that for a moment. Is there any fear that is keeping you from moving forward? Crippling you in any way?

If so, write it down, and then continue to read. God has some sweet lessons ahead, and oh, how we can rest assured God is bigger than our fear! God's authority over Satan is supreme and certain. Learning to join forces with God is one of the biggest reasons God allowed me to go through this journey.

Maybe if only to tell you about it.

The Bible describes this as war in the book of Ephesians:

"For our struggle is not against flesh and blood, but against the rulers, against the authorities, against the powers of this dark world and against the spiritual forces of evil in the heavenly realms." (Ephesians 6:12)

We have to learn to fight! Then learn to fight *well*!

First, for me, I had to learn to leave things that gave me that "creepy" feeling alone, to stay away from people that gave me that same bad taste in my mouth, and to run fast from evil lurking on the other side of a door. These are all good lessons to learn-

Especially until we learn how to fight!

A "good fear" I would call that now. A sixth sense, a learned response, and last but not least, it can be power of The Holy Spirit himself helping you and I out, protecting us.

The realization that I needed more equipping to fight the battle the book of Ephesians teaches us about started to form in my heart around the age of fourteen. I began to read my Bible more and more on my own. I paid more attention in church.

Almost every night I talked to God. I still enjoyed gazing out the window, appreciating the beauty of the night sky, praying for answers to every question a young teenager could think of. And boy, did I have some. And man, I still do. God, my Heavenly Father, still gets a kick out of all my questions. I am his kid and I just know that he thinks I am funny. Isn't it great that God knows us so well and just loves us!

I started longing to talk to someone about what I had been through as a kid. I wanted to make sense of it, and I also wanted to know if it had been real. I sure remembered it as being real and not a dream. But I wanted to be sure. I wanted understanding.

I, of course, also wanted to know "*why me?*"

Why would a child go through what I had went through?

Why would I have seen and felt what I saw and felt?

No one that I spoke with had had experiences with seeing things and feeling things that I had. Disbelief is what I received when I shared my stories, and it made people uncomfortable, again, like I had done something wrong, so I quit sharing. A couple more years passed, and I didn't mention anything to anyone.

I felt in my heart what I had seen, what I had heard, what I had experienced, was real. I knew God was real. I had felt his presence, and it was good. I decided that I wanted more of that, more of God's peace and goodness. I had a growing longing in my soul for more of God's love and more of his presence.

I still have that longing. I want still more. This story is about more. What do you want more of?

More love? More peace? More joy?

To be steadfast?

Yes, me too!

I want more of all of those things, God has it to give, and he wants to give it!

The Bible says to crave it:

"Like newborn babies, crave pure spiritual milk, so that by it you may grow up in your salvation, now that you have tasted that the Lord is good." (1Peter 2:2-3)

Have you found, like myself, that if you eat a lot of candy and cookies over the weekend, you want it all week? Man, my sweet tooth gets worse if it gets fed. But my soul gains more longing the more I feed it prayer, worship music and time reading my Bible. I was experiencing this feeding and this craving without realizing it.

Salvation in the terms of salvation was not mine yet. But I was craving the things of the Lord. I was growing up and indeed had tasted that the Lord was good.

The certainty I felt when I prayed was the same as when I was seven. God was real. God was present, and God heard me when I spoke to him.

Life was peaceful, sleep was sweet, and I had no reason to believe it would ever be anything different.

As I look at this period of time, I want to make certain I am not missing anything. I want to grow now even as I write this and rewrite and rewrite to get ready to share with others and be full in understanding for my own self.

What was going on? Why was I at peace?

Well, I was talking to God; relationship was being created between us. I was reading my Bible so I was forming opinions of what I was reading. I was attending church and listening. I was singing songs of praise, and this made my heart happy when I sang.

I find all of this to still be true.

There is still much to be said on spiritual alignment (doing what God would have us do) and God answering our prayers, our prayers matching his will, and I could go on and on.

But, seeking God, I continued to have peace. I was learning of his love, and I was looking for answers.

"Thank you, Heavenly Father, you promise to be with us and in front of us if we are seeking you!"

Our Heavenly Father promises us:

"For the LORD will go before you, And the God of Israel will be your rear guard."
Isaiah 52:12

"Come near to God and he will come near to you."
James 4:8

"You will seek me and find me when you seek me with all your heart."
Jeremiah 29:13

"I love those who love me, and those who seek me find me."
Proverbs 8:17

God is a light in a dark place. He is a light on a bright shiny day. His light is always able to push the darkness out. He is grace, and He is peace. He wants us to know this so deeply.

Slowly, I was getting this. The Bible says grace and peace comes through knowledge of God and Jesus Christ Our Lord.

Do you know what grace is? It is unearned favor! Undeserved reward! In the Bible, Peter explains that it can be ours IN ABUNDANCE through knowledge. We just have to pursue the knowledge!

Don't we all want an abundance of grace and peace?!

"Grace and peace be yours in abundance through the knowledge of God and Jesus Christ Our Lord."2 Peter 1:2

However, what had bothered me before still wanted to bother me. Fear still wanted to rattle my soul. I would find that out soon. Amongst the grace and peace, there was a war going on I did not know about.

Nor had I learned how to fight.

Personal Notes

4- "The Pursuit"

Now we travel from me as little girl
battling the darkness to recognizing that
God's light and Satan's darkness is all
around and believing God is stronger.
Believing that God's light is brighter
than the dark. I have grown up quite a
bit.

That little girl continued to learn to
leave things alone that gave her the
"heebie-jeebies." She is a Bible reader
and also a lover of the Psalms. She is
now a seventeen-year-old young woman
"head over heels" in love with her future
husband. She is still clueless as to why
her childhood has many memories of
horrible scary things in the night.

And still not actually a Christian.

When I use the word Christian, I mean
what is commonly called "being saved." I
had yet to be saved when Tommy (my
husband) and I started dating at 16 years
old. "Saved" meaning I had not had a
moment in time where I agreed with the
Good LORD Almighty that I was a sinner
and that I needed forgiveness as well as
His guidance. I had yet to have a

personal relationship with Jesus Christ that involved my surrender and his love.

My parents had taken me to church growing up. This included Sunday school and my summer time favorite-Vacation Bible School. I had a decent understanding of the Bible for my age. I believed in God. Remember, I had received His help. I trusted God. I prayed. I read my Bible all by myself most nights. But as I continued to get to know Tommy, I felt I was missing something.

When Tommy and I started dating at sixteen, I began attending church services with him. It was way, way, way, way different from mine. Did I say "way" enough times? I doubt it. Let me explain.

The church I attended with my family had a piano and an organ with music and preaching similar to most Independent Christian, Baptist or Methodist Churches at that time. We had messages from the Bible presented in a public speaking type of manner. We sang the old beautiful hymns such as "How Great Thou Art," "Washed in the Blood" and my favorite, "Standing on the Promises," from hymnals. It was pretty quiet. It was reverent; maybe subdued is also a good description, meaning a low spoken "Amen" might seem too loud. I am not saying this is bad; I liked our church.

I am saying I was shocked that church could be so very different from where I had always attended.

Tommy was part of *Fire Escape Ministries* in our hometown of Hartselle, Alabama. It was a small place full of teenagers and two great leaders, Charley and Shari Cain. Their huge hearts to see us teenagers grow in our faith was and still is amazing.

The Fire Escape was like nothing I had ever seen or even heard about (The internet didn't exist at that time.) This place had loud music! A band!!! I know bands are common in churches now (even my own) but not at the time, not thirty years ago. They had people clapping, people raising their hands and even an occasional shout! People would dance.

Dance!

I had never seen anything like it, and I was not sure I liked it. Uncomfortable is the word that comes to my mind the quickest and also judgement! "Who knew people could act like this at church?" I thought!

However, the preaching was relevant to what we were going through and scripture was used within context. Pastor Charley was interactive with us, asking us questions from the pulpit. He spoke more to us than at us. He wanted us to not just know the gospel but to understand it. I loved that.

Week after week, I got pretty hung up on the music and people's behavior. I had never really even sung in church much because it was so quiet in the sanctuary. But WOW- I thought this place was out of control! It was so loud!

Surely, God was not happy with their behavior! However, Tommy loved this place, and he was one of the crazy hand raisers all excited-on Sunday morning. And I did absolutely love that they were excited about God.

I longed for that excitement for myself!

I began my own Bible study, trying to find out if the reason for their "wild behavior" was in there. Maybe even to prove them wrong.

Well, it was there. Actually, it was all over the place. They were right in their behavior. I learned they were performing acts of praise.

In many scriptures, I found instances of people shouting to the Lord! People being encouraged to raise hands in prayer and the joy of the Lord during worship. It was throughout the Bible! In some scriptures it even speaks as a command for God's people to worship and pray with our hands raised!

<u>A couple of my favorites:</u>

"So I will bless you as long as I live; in your name I will lift up my hands." Psalm 63:4

"Lift up your hands in the sanctuary and praise the LORD!" Psalm 134:2

Now, I did not become a hand raiser immediately, but I did become a pursuer of this excitement and praise. I began to close my eyes in worship rather than watch others. This alone changed my entire world. Even in singing quietly with my eyes closed, I became a worshiper. A thankful heart for the music, a thankful heart for Tommy who was beside me, a thankful heart for being loved by God and my family.

With my eyes closed, I could allow myself to feel the worship, to feel the presence of God in a new way. I was choosing to worship; I was choosing to be a part.

This makes me feel old, but I will tell you anyway. Cassette tape radios, maybe some of you remember them, is what filled the dash of my car during this time. Tommy bought me a couple of cassette tapes with Christian music on them. My little grey Nissan car became a vehicle of praise.

On the way to school in the mornings, I learned to sing my heart out to God.

Never, ever underestimate the little things you sow into another's life! I crack up as I write this, thinking how awesome it is that Tommy was sowing into his future wife!
But also, how much more he probably would have done if he knew he was going to live with me forever!

That really is funny and probably true!

Ok, let's go back to 1990!

Alone in my car, I gave myself freedom to sing out loud, and sometimes too loudly. Freedom to sing the words from my heart to God. To sing over and over the verses of the songs.

And it felt as if God were singing them back to me. My heart learned to rejoice in His love and in music!

And my Spirit learned to sing with The Holy Spirit!

If you have never pursued God in worship, do it today! He created us for it! We were born to worship! Worship can bring more joy than anything else, and even if it doesn't, we were still created for it and told to do it! It really is a joy though!

Here are a couple more things The Bible says about worshiping:

Psalm 100 says:
"Shout for joy to the LORD, all the earth. Worship the LORD with gladness; come before him with joyful songs. Know that the LORD is God. It is he who made us, and we are his; we are his people the sheep of his pasture."

**Romans 5:8 gives us reason to worship:
"But God demonstrates his own love for us in this: While we were still sinners, Christ died for us."**

Learning to praise changed my life; it changed my heart and my view of everything around me!

Bible studies during the weeknights became common with our friends from The Fire Escape. We discussed everything. I mean everything. Thankfully, one couple

in our group was older and wiser. Because
I had a lot of questions. Questions about
Jesus, The Holy Spirit, different
churches, angels, spirits, music, death.

Questions. Boy, did I have questions.

Because it seemed everything that came
out of Pastor Charley Cain's mouth was
new information to me in this
questioning. I know a large part of this
was because I was listening for the first
time as a grown person, a grown person
asking God to help them understand.

Pastor Charley spoke of the Holy Spirit.
A lot it seemed. I was a lot clueless
about The Holy Spirit. I couldn't
remember much ever being taught about The
Holy Spirit. Maybe that is why it seemed
like a lot, or perhaps my mind and heart
had just finally matured enough to
understand what I had actually heard all
my life.

Communion had been a weekly part of
service in my church growing up. They,
not me, (This was for baptized
believers,) took the communion wafer and
communion juice, ate it and drank it –
"In the Name of the Father, the Son and
The Holy Spirt." That was all I really
had in my memory about The Holy Spirit.
And I did not understand it. But I wanted
to.

I felt a greater longing but did not realize it was The Holy Spirit creating that greater longing in my heart to know God. To want to know Him more. To know Jesus. To know The Holy Spirit. I longed to receive The Holy Spirit's help in all things in my life, so the pursuit of what was real and true about God and life continued!

But then, just like that- "IT" was back-BAM!!! Once again, I was being pursued by something not of God.

Something was in my room.

Every fiber of my being knew it wasn't a "someone." What it was-was something I wished was not there! A demon? A foul spirit? a ghost? I was not certain what to name it. But the same type of scary presence from when I was very young had returned. I could not scream. I could not even move. Seventeen years old and back where I was at seven. My most intimate place, my bedroom, was being invaded.

Again.

What I could see was something dark and fuzzy across the room, a form, but I couldn't focus on it. I could hear it!

Like hearing a hiss of a snake and heavy breathing muffled through a microphone all at once. Oh, how I longed to scream and scream loud. How I wanted to cry out for help! I had no voice! I wanted to scream just to be screaming!

Even more I wanted this to go away and never, ever come back!

Over the next two or three months, I experienced seeing things moving around in the dark of my room. I experienced being so afraid I could hardly breathe even though I could not see what I could feel. The terror always felt it would never end. I feared for my life, not understanding what was going on.

Dreams of demons, of red eyes in the dark, were becoming very common. Visions of darkness in my dream world would awaken me breathless. Then while waking, I would feel the same sense of foulness from long ago. My sleep was being invaded, my bedroom was being invaded, and it seemed it was all closing in on me. The war was back on, and I was losing ground quickly.

I'd like to tell you that I returned to the 23rd Psalm and just handled this with the word of God, but I didn't. I somehow didn't even think to do that! I was

focused on what I was scared of and
obviously not thinking straight!

What I did was change bedrooms.

I know that was crazy, stupid really,
like changing bedrooms could actually
make a difference. But that is what I
did. I moved into the other bedroom
upstairs, the smaller one, because all
teenagers want a smaller bedroom… Ummmm.
No. Because I thought maybe I could leave
that darkness, evil, demon-whatever it
was-in the other room.

Wrong.
It came with me, following me right out
one door and into the other.

If only I would have remembered those 5
steps from Chapter One!

Crazy dreams of people dying, me unable
to help them, dreams of people fighting.
I particularly dreamed a lot of being
trapped in an old house all alone. This
at least made sense. I felt like I was
because I was the only one in our house
who was hearing things, seeing things and
totally scared out of their wits.

Broken, tired and confused with it all, I
confessed to Tommy (same boyfriend and
future husband) what was going on. What I
was afraid of and how fear had been

making "appearances" in my room. I figured he, too, would think I was crazy or making it up, but he didn't think either of those things.

That night on the phone (one of those old ones that connected to the wall for those of you that remember those) he started the conversation of being saved.

We discussed my relationship with God and his. I knew of God, about God. I even talked to God. I believed in God, but I had not made that decision to be part of his kingdom. I felt and knew in that moment that I had not connected to God in the way he was talking about.

I still remember my heart beat picking up when Tommy asked me if I wanted to be saved. I wasn't completely clear on what that all meant but my soul longed for it. I knew that Tommy's relationship with God was better than what I had. I wanted more, whatever he needed to name it. Salvation! Sign me up!

I said yes!

I smile as I write that. This man has given me the two best gifts that came with questions. The first question "Are you saved?" followed with prayer and help in receiving the gift of salvation through Jesus Christ. The second big

question was "Will you marry me?" offered
with his heart and ring in hand for me to
become his wife.

Thank you, Tommy, if you ever do read
this. You are really the best friend a
person could have and the best husband a
woman could ask for. I love you with all
my heart. Thank you for your love and
continuous concern for me. You are my
helpmate sent from God.

Tommy prayed, and I repeated what he
said. Simple words were said like-"
Father God, forgive me. I am a sinner.
Jesus, I know you died to save me! I
accept your forgiveness and Holy Spirit.
Come into my life and change me from the
inside out. Amen."

I felt lighter. I cried. And then cried
some more.

I was overcome with so much joy! It was a
beautiful moment where God connected my
heart to His in a new way. I received
God, Jesus and The Holy Spirit! I felt
like all my troubles were over and I even
thought the events I had been dealing
with at night would be forever gone.

Well, the part about connecting my heart
to God still stands. The events that
showed up in my bedroom, well that went
from bad to worse.

Who knew it even could? Not me. But that is exactly what happened.

Makes me think of a couple of sayings I have heard many times,

"Sometimes things have to get worse before they get better."
or
"What doesn't kill you makes you stronger."

Ughhhh.

How about this instead?

"Look to the LORD and his strength; seek his face always." 1 Chronicles 16:11

"Those who know your name trust in you, for you, LORD, have never forsaken those who seek you." Psalm 9:10

"But those whose hope is in the LORD will renew their strength. They will soar on wings like eagles, they will run and not grow weary, they will walk and not faint." Isaiah 40:31

And even better this awesome verse from the Book of Jeremiah:

The LORD appeared to us in the past, saying:

"I have loved you with an everlasting love; I have DRAWN you with unfailing kindness."

You see, we are all being drawn to God. I was being drawn and pursued by God in all that despair and fear. I was seeking and God was drawing me close. God was growing me and teaching me.

I am thankful that God's love will never run dry! Not now, not ever, not for any of us!

His pursuit of us started before we were born!

Personal Notes

5- "Light in The Dark"

Just so we are clear-At this point in my story, I am now saved. I am washed in the blood of the Lamb, a sinner saved by grace, and I am learning how to praise God for all of it at The Fire Escape. I am reading my Bible and loving God with what I know so far. So, what is going on? Why on God's beautiful earth is this trouble back?

Because it was back and back with a vengeance!

Who wants to awaken feeling like they have a pillow on their face? No one! Yet, without asking for it, in my smaller bedroom, I had the exact same experience as before. Several times.

I became so scared of the dark-again. I hated turning off the light. Turn on the light to go up the stairs; turn it on to go down. I left a light on every chance I got-the bathroom light, the closet light, the overhead light. But it didn't matter; it did not keep the fear from rising inside me, and it did not keep it from manifesting itself in physical or spiritual form.

Lights on or lights off, when the dark presence showed up, all I could focus on was it. I always felt it before I saw it. What was it going to do? Was it going to kill me this time? I felt certain it wanted to.

Then doubt of my salvation came. Why? Why is this happening? Where was this Holy Spirit I was learning about? Was I really saved?

Surely, I was not saved I thought. That is what this is about.

I went forward at a youth worship night. When they called for prayer at the front, I close to ran up there, asking to be saved. I unloaded on the person who came to pray with me. They asked me questions about my salvation experience and then assured me that I had done my part and that God was doing His. I told them about what was going on in my bedroom at night and my horrific nightmares and that surely, I wasn't saved. What kind of saved girl has Satan trying to get her in her own room over and over again?

They were so encouraging, explaining how Satan wanted to come against those who oppose him, those not on his team. They explained how fear was stealing my peace and prayed scripture over me. They had a few others come and place their hands on me and pray over me, and I felt a new sense of calmness wash over me. I cried and cried, but I felt the certainty of what had been said was true. But goodness, what a mess I was in this growing process.

Isaiah 26:3 explains this as each of us keeping our minds set on God for peace and trusting in God. I again was focused on the wrong thing, the presence and my fear, not on what God could do.

I haven't a clue who that was that I spoke to that night, but I am thanking God for them again as I write this. They were used to change my life.

The words they spoke were true and simple. For me to ask God to protect me and to search the Bible and read what it says about fear and protection. That those things were written for me and everyone like me. I immediately remembered the 23rd Psalm as they spoke. How could I have forgotten something so powerful? So important? So simple?

Well, that's easy! Because Satan comes to steal, to kill and destroy all that is good and against him (John 10:10). That goodness was kept hidden from me. I had somehow not remembered that Psalm. Isn't that crazy? But the moment I remembered it, I remembered it word for word. Amazing!

The rest of that particular scripture in John 10:10 tells us that Jesus came so we could have life and have it to the full. God wants us to have the best life ever! Full of all the goodness he has for each of us! But it is our choice what we focus on!

As I shifted my focus, I started looking for God's promises about protection.

In the 23rd Psalm God's word promises He is with us!

We are promised in Proverbs 3:24 "When you lie down, you will not be afraid; when you lie down your sleep will be sweet."

Psalm 4:8 promised me, "In peace I will lie down and sleep, for you alone, Lord, make me dwell in safety."

I loved that one!

In peace I could lie down-God would keep me safe!

I began reading these over and over again at night. With my new found assurance of God's word, I slept for several weeks without an incident. Sweet dreamless sleeping. I woke overjoyed that the night had come and gone without terror.

I was learning my Bible in a new way. What was in it was not just my hope; the promises were my weapons.
I was learning to understand that I could trust what God had spoken to the people who wrote the Bible. I was learning He was speaking to me through reading it.

Then one night I was right back where I had been so many times. You are probably thinking, "Really? Really, Tina?"

Yes, really.

There I was-awake. Frozen in fear. Eyes wide open. Something powerful was keeping me from moving. Fear. Fear so big in me I could not speak or cry out. As if a hand was around my throat, I was gasping for air. Movement and noises coming from all different parts of my room. Overhead there was racket. To my right and to my left. Movement and little noises as if my furniture was being moved around in the room.

A horror movie script could not have made this any more frightening. The room seemed to become so dark; and yet, at my door, where the light of the bathroom should have been shining, was even more darkness, a presence.

The presence was several feet in height, almost as tall as my door. (Notice that- "at the door".) Regardless of the attack Satan's crappy darkness had moved away from me even further!

I wish I had noticed this years ago! It wasn't until I started journaling and reading my old journals to get this all in a book that I noticed the difference. God's power is in that! His power is in you and me. It is in the strength of His word being planted, watered and grown in our hearts. Even as weak as I was in my faith, what I was experiencing had still moved!

So, in this moment, with fear all over me and the biggest version of darkness I had seen so far approaching me, I started to pray out loud and tell God that I am counting on that verse about not being fearful because He is with me. I will lie down. I will not be afraid. I will be safe. I will FEAR NO EVIL. Jesus is with me. I belong to God! He will fight for me!

I remember getting even more scared while praying. I felt it made the presence mad because something felt different. At that moment I only knew I was more afraid than ever. It was as if I could hear it roaring in my ears.

Then-I remember very specifically, very clearly asking Jesus to come and remove it.

But even better, I remember as clearly as if it happened just now what happened next!

Light flooded my bedroom!

Instantly! Yes! Instantly! Bright light! Blinding white light! Brilliant radiant light!

My upstairs bedroom appeared to have car lights shining in from two of the three windows. My bedroom was that lit up! There is and was no explanation other than God's presence!

It was amazing! Peace, beautiful peace, wrapped around me like a blanket. Beautiful joy, a visible and almost touchable presence of God. His Light! I was so thankful for that light and the feeling of assurance that was in my heart. I am still so thankful for that moment. The presence at the door was gone by the power of God!

Good over evil! Light over dark and faith over fear. Wow. I was amazed. What had just happened? It lasted moments: yet, I am still in awe.

I received in this particular moment, while praying what the Bible already promises to be true and receiving prayer from others, complete triumph in Jesus and with God. Victory over this form of evil, this form of darkness, this visible fear. Gone! Swiftly! Easily and softly! Brilliantly! Beautifully and powerfully!

An ocean of calmness just washing over me! Perfect peace like a gentle breeze. God's protection like I had never known.

Beautiful beyond words.

God never meant for us to do life alone. My relationship with God was growing. Learning and even just beginning to understand God's love for me was changing everything.

Allowing others who were wiser than myself to speak/counsel me was a growth point. I am thankful for that and for having friends pray for me. The power in other believers praying with me and for me was and is significant.

Some battles require more fighters than others to win, especially if the one being targeted is not that strong. Let us all remember that whether we are the weak one needing prayer or whether we are the

strong one praying for our brother or
sister in need.

I especially love the prayer Paul prayed
for his fellow believers in the Book of
Colossians 1:9-13.

**"For this reason also, we have not ceased to pray
for you and to ask that you may filled with the
knowledge of his will in all spiritual wisdom and
understanding, so that you may walk in a manner
worthy of the Lord, to please him in all respects,
bearing fruit in every good work and increasing in
the knowledge of God; strengthened with all
power, according to His glorious might, for the
attaining of all steadfastness and patience; joyously
giving thanks to the Father, who has qualified us to
share in the inheritance of the saints of Light. For
He rescued us from the domain of darkness, and
transferred us to the kingdom of His beloved son."**

Transferred to the Kingdom of Light! We
CAN be rescued from darkness!

Just Wow! Doesn't that just make you want
to be a part of it all?

It did me! But it still had me asking why
I had the experiences? I now understood
that what I felt and seen as a child was
indeed real-one important question
answered.

But why? Why did I feel that dark presence? Why did I hear noises that no-one else in the house heard? Why did I see what I saw?

Was it only so God could show me how victorious He is? Was it so I could learn the realness of God? Was I somehow pursuing the wrong thing? Was I somehow inviting this in?

Then even bigger questions. Was this a demon? What was a demon? Why would I have a demon in my room? Why would anyone? Now that I had God's assurance of safety, I became braver in my questions.

More Bible study revealed to me that demons are the fallen angels who followed Satan in his rebellion against God and are now evil spirits under Satan's control. Satan and his demons are here to destroy our peace, distort the truth of the gospel, rock our faith, hinder salvation and bring darkness where there can be light.

The history of Satan is very simple actually. Isaiah 14:12-15 explains that Satan rebelled against God, that he wanted to reign higher than God and God removed him and his followers from the Heavens.

Satan exists; his demons also exist. However, if we look at the big picture of demons in The Bible, it is about casting them out, overcoming them and moving on. The focus is not about their destructive natures. It is not about what they can and cannot do. It is not about what they do or do not look like.

The truth of The Bible, in reference to Satan and his helpers, is about us having Jesus on our side. With the power of God, we need not fear Satan's power because Satan's power is limited.

And God's power is not limited in any way.

God's power created Heaven and Earth. God's power created us and can help us in all areas of our lives.

God wants us to understand this ongoing spiritual war between good and evil, between himself and Satan (see Matthew 12:43-45). And God wants us to choose to be on his side and win!

Again, it comes back to focus. We cannot deny Satan's existence, but the overcoming is in the focus. God is all powerful and if we belong to him and choose his promises over anything Satan brings at us, we will not be defeated.

I had landed right back where I was at seven, learning and agreeing with what God's word says. God had taught me a new grown-up perspective of accepting it and standing firm in it.

The Bible is very clear that Satan and his demons lose all their power when they are controlled by Jesus or the power of His Name. I wanted to be certain I understood this part. Jesus merely spoke the word "Go" to the demons mentioned in Matthew Chapter 8, and they went.

Paul, a follower and teacher of Christianity in The New Testament, showed us our personal authority in Christ. It is just as simple. Paul spoke directly to a demon in Acts 16:18, saying, "In the name of Jesus Christ, I command you to come out of her!" And at that moment the spirit left her.

This made me think, "What does it mean to have the authority of Christ?" I wondered what it meant to say- "In the name of Jesus."

So back to The Bible I went! Authority means power, like a police officer has the power to arrest me if I commit a crime. God's authority is his right or power to command and enforce obedience. This made sense. God has the power over

Satan, Jesus has power over Satan, Paul
had power over Satan and his demons and
through my relationship with God, I have
the power over Satan.

But what about the phrase "In the name of
Jesus?" I think that at seventeen I truly
only understood this to mean by whom are
you doing this, why are you doing this-
that there was power in Jesus and his
name. This is true and made a solid step
in my faith.

But a few years back, I had to have
written permission to hunt a piece of
property. I had to carry it at all times
while hunting. The slim slip of paper
said that I, Tina Sims, had Henry
Patterson's (my Daddy) permission to hunt
his land. Dad had signed it and dated it
in case I was ever stopped by the game
warden. This "written permission" is a
good idea, but it is also a law
requirement in the state I hunt in.

One day, as I sat in my tree stand
waiting on a deer to walk by, I
envisioned being stopped and asked on my
way out of the woods, "By whose
permission do you have to hunt on this
land?" I could see myself happily getting
my "permission slip" out, quickly telling
that person by whose authority I had
received the right to do what I was
doing. The Land Owners, that's who! And

the fact that I am the Land Owner's daughter adds even more punch doesn't it?

Something fabulous clicked and authority from Heaven took on a whole new meaning for me! As Christ followers we have a "permission slip" from the Land Owner of Heaven to Earth to do work with His full authority! Our territory is God's territory!

We have the right to do what He would do!

We are God's kids!

There are so many scriptures on all of this. Here are some to start with:

Of God's power, we can read Jeremiah Chapter 32-
"Ah Sovereign LORD, you have made the heavens and the earth by your great power and outstretched arm. Nothing is too hard for you."

In Matthew 28:18, we are told of Christ's authority.
It reads, "Then Jesus came to them and said,
'All authority in heaven and on earth has been given to me.'"

And of our authority in Christ,
"For everyone who has been born of God overcomes the world. And this is the victory that has overcome the world-our faith. Who is it that overcomes the world except the one who believes that Jesus is the Son of God?" 1 John 5:4-5

Then I began to learn to rejoice in belonging to God, having forgiveness through Jesus, and understanding authority within that.

1 Peter 2:9 encourages us that we are a chosen people, a royal priesthood, a holy nation, a people belonging to God, so that we may declare the praises of him who's called us out of the darkness into his wonderful light!

And God's light shines in the darkness and the darkness has not overcome it! John 1:5

Oh, the joy of growing closer to God! I was learning then, and I am still learning now!

I was still asking, "why?" I did not get an answer then, and as I continue to ponder this question; I truly think it is part personality and part attack. As we journey through life our personality makes us more available to things that bring us joy and things that bring us sadness, based on what we perceive as fun or beautiful or good. Our emotions play a factor in how we receive everything; and I believe I was still receiving through a receptor of fear.

I can recall watching a movie during this time called "Hell's Bells." It was about Satanic motives behind music. Did it frighten me? Yes. Disturb me? Yes. Did it bother anyone else in the room watching it?
I really do not think it did. The conversation after it was logical and opinionated, not fear based and not focused on Satan or his demons, unlike myself.

So, had I cracked the door open again? Maybe I had; maybe I hadn't. Perhaps, it was just a spiritual attack. Or maybe even a test.

However, based on past experiences, we can all have negative experiences reoccur and rattle us until we understand it and master it with God's word. I was learning to master it even if I didn't get the *why* at that time.

Life doesn't always make sense. What happens to us doesn't always make sense. And you know what? Everything of God has not always made sense and still does not always make sense to me. But growing a sense of certainty within a world that doesn't make sense-makes sense!

And for me that still looks the same-very, very good!

<u>Personal Notes</u>

6- "Faith Over Fear"

I would love to tell you that was it…The
End. The end of "The Ugly."

More than 20 years passed without a dark
story to tell.

I thought this was complete having been
through what I perceived as so much
seemed pretty remarkable. In seeing God's
supernatural light, God's beauty and
receiving supernatural help, I thought
the story was finished, complete and
ready to share.

But God had some more to teach me;
imagine that.
He always does.

I'd like to tell you that I had it all
figured out and have walked victoriously
and faithfully with the Lord ever since
those teenage years, but that would be a
big fat lie.

I struggled with wanting to feel like I
was good enough to even be called a
Christian for a long time. Where I
arrived to as a teenager, I lingered.

Saved. I was saved. I understood that and
I had learned to praise and enjoy God's

presence, but I also walked side by side with the agony of not feeling "good enough." It felt like a lot of two steps forward and three steps back, another strategy from the enemy I did not understand.

Growing in faith is a lifetime journey and can look very different for each of us. I spent years more focused on doing everything right rather than cultivating my relationship with God. And that proved too hard. I should have been focusing on growing my relationship and my faith in that.

Faith is defined as complete trust in someone or something. We often learn to trust by needing it, like trusting your brakes to stop you at a stop sign. We use them. They work. We trust them each time we push the pedal.

We can't quite compare God to a set of brakes, but we do trust our car's brakes the more we consistently use them, and they prove to do what brakes were designed for.

Did I trust God? Yes. Did I trust God? No. I have been both of those. Some promises in the Bible were difficult to learn to trust. Some I did not even know. But mostly, I still spent a lot of years trying to trust me.

I wrecked myself with my thoughts, "Did I pray enough? Did I attend church enough? Should I serve more at church? Was my devotional time long enough? Was I a good wife? Could I be a better employee?"

Into my late twenties, I had returning thoughts that possibly I wasn't saved. I didn't always feel saved, and I sure made a lot of mistakes. I struggled with wanting to be the best wife and wanting Tommy to be more of a Godly husband.

At one period in time, it would even have appeared that I gave up the pursuit of my relationship with God, and did whatever I wanted. I never gave up the pursuit of God but I did do a lot I can't take back.

"Religion," "church," "and being a Christian" often just felt like it was too hard.

I had yet to understand walking in faith and grace. God offered it, and I had yet to accept it completely. Thankfully, God's pursuit was better than mine and better than Satan's had ever been. *Thank you, Father God! We can receive you completely.*

With lives packed full of good and bad decisions, God still loves us endlessly!

Let me say that again-God loves you endlessly! God's promises are amazing!

I have accepted the promise in 2 Corinthians 12:9:

"My grace is sufficient for you, for my power is made perfect in weakness".

Did you get that? God's power is made perfect in our weakness!
Sign me up!

God's grace is sufficient! This means God's grace is ENOUGH!

Grace is defined as the freely given love of God. Freely given! At no cost, at no merit and at no work do we receive God's love. This is grace. He already loves us. We just have to receive it! We CANNOT earn it.

It took me a while on that one.

But I now know that is where faith is built, in accepting God's love along with trust in Jesus as our Savior and in learning that what God commands is actually the best thing for us.

And faith did take me some time to develop.

But God has developed it and will continue to do so.

My thirties and forties have been spent growing in that relationship. Time changes so much about us, but there is much to be said about "what goes in, comes out."

Reading the Bible and being part of worship, church and relationship with God continues to change me, to complete what He started.

I still make mistakes, but like gold being refined, our lives are a process. It's about living in relationship with God, and in doing that I have become one of the happiest people I know!

Having God so close in my daily life really is a joy. God is growing me in boldness in prayer, discussing my faith in person and in writing, and the blessings are endless.

The life God has given me is a life better than I truly could have imagined for myself.

I do still sense evil or darkness in people and places, and it is now teaching me how to pray more effectively. It is continuously leading me how to ask and listen to God with what is going on around me.

This does not make me more special. We are all special! Every single one of us were designed to have a close relationship with our Father in Heaven. How close of a relationship we have is up to us.

Knowing there is more relationship to be had, more wisdom to receive, and more encouragement God can give me to give to others and apply to my day, excites me! Regardless of the fact that I am not perfect! Regardless of the fact that I do not have it all figured out!

I have learned to talk to God in all my fears and give it to him, a journey of learning what my favorite hymn "Standing on the Promises" really means.

Getting to know God has brought me to a point of wanting to please God. This is very different than me trying to check off a to do list each week of how long I spent at church or how much I studied my Bible or whether I did or didn't say or do the wrong thing.

I wish I knew how to explain this to a seventeen-year-old. I sure could have used this conversation. Perhaps, only life could have taught it to me based on

what I had been taught and what was being
taught. Regardless, please never give up!
Go to God, our Heavenly Father, and ask
him what He thinks. Read his word and
look for what He says!

One of the greatest things I have learned
is to ASK, *"God-what would you have me to
do?" and having HIM answer is even
better!*

There is a lot to be said as we ask God
that question, such as learning to align
myself with what God would want so I
could hear Him better, and the
willingness to do it. But even in the
pursuit of that (which will be a
continual journey in faith until I die),
there is the asking.

So, I encourage you to ask God whatever
is on your heart!

All of that being said, we get to right
now. We get to *me*, a grown-up-writing a
book. That sweet voice in my spirit
brought me to writing about my experience
with fear and how God is teaching me to
overcome with His help.

One evening late at night as I lay in bed
talking to God, I asked Him, "LORD, what
else would you have me to do?" God spoke
to me in my heart and mind, in a gentle
whisper. I heard, "I want you to write a

book." Now, He didn't say a good book or a great book, nor a best seller, just "a book."

Although, I would like to write a best seller (who wouldn't). I only knew that God wanted me to share what I know about fear. The visual appearance of fear, nightmares, evil spirits, disturbances and such. That those things were real and existed.

And that God is indeed bigger than whatever comes against us….

I thought the story was in the sharing about that. It is. It was. But for me it is so much more, the growth that came from Him speaking that He wanted me to write about it until now. God was still teaching me to overcome it. To get past it-for good.

He was still teaching me to align my life with His truth from the Bible, consistently.

Consistently, complete trust in God's word.

I did not realize at the time that I started writing this that there was so much left to learn. I know that is arrogant. I am sorry. I was wrong. But I did not think for a minute this journey would take me back to places I thought I had overcome.

Back to nights full of nightmares. Back to seeing and hearing things in the dark. Right back to fear that leaves you breathless and unresponsive.

But it did. Thankfully, God was with me in the next part of this story just like the last. He is behind us, beside us and in front of us!

God is good, and God is faithful. I am thankful of where I am now and thankful and trustful of where God will take me next.

God always wants to grow us more and more!

There is a verse in Jeremiah that tells us:
That if we call out to God, He will answer us and He will tell us great and unsearchable things that we do not know.

I love this verse.

God has proven it time and time again. I asked Him for help with writing down what I went through with this entire fear conversation.

So, I indeed called out to God.

However, I NEVER expected, after what I had seen of God's glory, to have any type of dark presence actually return. For it be in my home again. My home is my territory! OUR territory! GOD'S territory!

I expected wisdom in my mind as I wrote! Not distress in my house!

But there I was, as much of a grown-up as a grown person can be, not a child in person or in my faith in my Heavenly Father. I was not pursuing anything of Satan or the occult.

I was just trying to put together the thoughts and facts of what you have read so far in writing. Pursuing God, I am growing closer to My Lord and Savior daily even in the journey of writing it.

Perfect? No! Got it all figured out? No! But am I bringing the darkness upon me by negative behavior, fearful thoughts or occult actions? No!

Truthfully, I thought the experience I had at seventeen would be the last even when God asked me to write about it, even as I thought I was almost finished writing a short story about it.

That last visit with visible darkness in my home, God blessed it. God showed up and showed out, wrapping me in his light, such assurance over fear.

The end.

Well......No.

Again.

Again-I woke to that same fear! Something was in my room! OUR bedroom! My married-to-Tommy bedroom! I could feel the presence, the dread, the heaviness, the excessive darkness.

Immediately, I sat straight up in bed, trying to recognize if I was dreaming. Awake, I was awake! It was still there! My breathing became very shallow, I couldn't swallow, fear growing in me with every breath I took.

Married at eighteen, Tommy and I and have more than twenty-five years together at this point. None of them included a fearful visit. None of them!
Our home has been a peaceful place most of our married years, especially the last fifteen years as we have focused on putting God and each other before ourselves.

I think- *"What is going on!"* I am afraid
to move and my mind is racing! *"This
should not be happening! Command it out,
Command it out, command it out!"* My mind
screams from within!

I knew what I had to do. I had to command
it out, exercising the authority I have
because of my relationship with Jesus.

In that moment, I remembered what I knew
about authority, the same authority that
Jesus has over demons and spiritual
darkness and what I had seen for myself.
But as I stared at this large dark form,
I was also thinking- *"THIS SHOULDN'T BE
HAPPENING!"*

Then I saw it move about a foot. It was
coming toward me!

Sitting there in bed, my eyeballs were
straining to see and comprehend. I wanted
to see it. Every detail I wanted to see.
Even scared, I still wanted to see. I was
writing this book and could not remember
exact details from years before so I
wanted to see that what I remembered was
true and correct.

Yet, there really weren't any details.
Fear still looked the same. A dark or
evil presence is just a dark or evil
presence. The seeing of something

supernaturally evil now did not have any more details than I remembered as a kid or as a teenager. This same darkness still looked like a fog, a cloud, and a shadow all rolled into one.

Yet, the feeling of evil intention seemed worse.

And I was still scared to pieces of it.

As I sat and stared with my heart sounding off in my ears, I attempted to say something authoritative like, "Get out in the Name of Jesus!" Suddenly, my head and neck felt like they were in a vice. My head couldn't turn and pain radiated in my neck as I strained to move it. I was having difficulty drawing a breath. I fought to push air out of my throat and attempted to speak "Get out in the Name of Jesus!" again.

But I couldn't.

I knew what I wanted to say, the words were in my head; they just wouldn't come out of my mouth!

This was serious; now I no longer wanted to get any of those details. I had expected it to vanish with my authority

and all. Wrong again. I was thinking too
highly of myself; I suppose!

The darkness seemed neither male nor
female. It really was more like a shape
and smoke. Evil - that part was certain.
Mean and hateful, I could feel that. It
took three tries for me to speak at all,
but as soon as I did, it was quick to
disappear.

My boldness was growing in my heart each
time I tried to speak because I was
calling on God in my heart at the same
time. Focusing on God… was what worked
and even though my speech was garbled,
words running together, it still went
away.

My room brightened, and I could see
clearly again. The presence knew the
authority of Christ's name even as I
mumbled and stumbled with it. As the air
returned to my lungs, the heaviness in
the room disappeared. I laid down and
thanked God for HIS presence and HIS
peace, HIS goodness and HIS power.

I didn't ask why again.

I knew why.

I knew that in trying to understand the
terror from my past and getting it ready

to share, I was opening stuff back up. I was receiving a direct attack of the enemy. Recognizing that changed everything.

I then began having a lot of different dreams, dreams of my childhood home and dreams of my childhood friends. I had been looking for answers to why those encounters had happened to me as a child. I wanted to understand it. I was reading a couple of books on dream interpretation. I had been reading everything the Bible said about demons, on authority over demons, on fear, on peace, on protection and deliverance.

I wanted to write this story well. I was pursuing hard; understanding was showing up. I suppose the enemy thought he would too. Grown-up spiritual warfare.

I knew God was allowing it, allowing me to learn even as I was hating every minute. That verse in Jeremiah about calling out and God telling us things we don't know was taking on new meaning.

I knew that my faith in my beliefs was being tested and tried. I was in the pot like the gold that is boiled to become pure. I, too, was being refined in my understanding of God's power and in having the impurities in my faith skimmed off.

Now, I had new insight to Proverbs
Chapter 3:

**"Trust in the LORD with all your heart and lean
not on your own understanding; in all your ways
submit to him and he will make your paths
straight."**

None of this made complete sense, but
calling out to God in prayer did and will
always create an uprising in your Spirit
if you align it with His will.

I promised God I was willing to do
whatever He wanted me to do as long as He
made it very clear.

A straight path, a path with a view of
where I was going, came in to sight.

Personal Notes

7- "War Wages On"

Bad dreams, dreams that left me gasping, soaking in sweat and tears, picked up speed after this. Blood, terror, death-I was fighting in my sleep night after night.

Once, I dreamed I was in a public place and a dark spirit was trying to overtake me. It was so close to me I couldn't scream as if I was inside of a dark shadow unable to get out! Then I felt like it was inside of me as if I had swallowed the darkness! The pressure on the inside of me was killing me.

I was trying to move but I could not even wiggle. I was attempting to scream for help but could not. I wanted the others in the room to look at me not just to help me but to see that what I had been telling them was real!

But no one would even look my way. I then asked God to help me.

Then, easily, I was able to speak. I said something like "Leave me alone in Jesus's Name." And it was gone.

Alone.

This dream helped me understand sometimes
 we have to stand alone and call on God.
It helped me understand God would always
see and always be ready to help. I also
saw myself wanting others to understand
the reality of what I knew to be true.
For this story to line up with truth and
everyone who reads it to understand my
heart and even more-God's heart!

I prayed for more discernment. I wanted
to understand what every dream and every
encounter meant. I wanted to grow my
strength and relationship with God, My
Father. And trust me I still wanted all
the evil to stop.

New dreams came.

Bam! Bam! Bam! Someone was knocking on my
back door. Through the window I could see
not one, but several men standing on my
back porch. Like the FBI had shown up to
get me, all black suits and ties, except
one.

The man, appearing to be in charge of
them, was different. He was dressed in
white from head to toe, even had a white
hat on. Picture this man with a Boss Hog
looking outfit (from "The Dukes of
Hazard"-an old but wonderful TV show) on

a John Wayne type of fellow. Big man, big hat, big suit and in charge.

I cracked the back door open and asked what this was about. They were not smiling. Paperwork was presented to me declaring what was next from the boss in the white suit.

"What?" I say, trying to grasp what was going on. The white suit fellow said that I was to be arrested and have all of our belongings and our home taken!

I began panicking, heart pounding, trying to think of who I could call. Trying to think of what to do. I stood holding the door that blocked the entrance… and paused and prayed. I closed my eyes for just a moment and asked God to give me wisdom. "Help God… wisdom." I whispered quickly.

I had not done anything wrong!

I opened my eyes and looked right at the man dressed in white. My hand came off the door, and I pushed it open. Shoulders straight, head up, I walked out on my porch. After prayer I knew he was a fraud!

Looking directly at the man in white, I said, "I command you to leave my home by the authority of Jesus Christ!" I was shaking, and I was screaming!

I couldn't believe it as I watched…. The men, all of them, turned and walked away without a word. Not one of them even looked back at me, not a word, into their vehicles they went. A white SUV for the lead man, black SUV's for the others and out of my drive way they rolled.

Wow, it was weird. The dream seemed so real like the real FBI or Police had shown up and I had spoken to them in that manor. Like the authorities really would have left if this had happened and commanded them to leave by the authority of Christ. The earthly police would not, but in my dream, they each turned away without saying another word and got in their vehicles and left my home.

But they were not earthy police, and not everything we fight is of this world.

Once again, God was showing me and you that we are not always fighting a battle that makes earthly sense. Once again, in the spiritual realm God was showing me no matter how big and bad the situation is- we still have victory in Jesus. We not only have authority, but we can also have boldness. We are strong enough if we seek God's help. Prayer is our lifeline!

Storing God's word in our hearts and minds is what we fight with!

THIS IS FAITH! Complete trust in God for a situation, for our very lives!

Even when my legs are shaking!

John 10:10 tells us-

"Satan comes to steal, kill and destroy. But Jesus came that we may have life and have it to the full."

Lying in bed, in the aftermath of this dream, I thought of that scripture and what it meant in relationship to this dream.

I certainly do not want to stand by and have Satan take anything from me in any form. I do not wish to invite him into my home to give him what doesn't belong to him. I want to watch for him and stand with God's authority for what God promises.

You must understand; I was overwhelmed with this dream. It was a WOW kind of dream for me. So real and so important as I journeyed through writing this book. God was warning me and encouraging me. Again, God was showing me His Authority and my authority in him through Jesus.

Not only was He able, I was too.

I could go on and on about the details in this dream we could learn from because I know I am still learning from it. God, our Heavenly Father, is the best teacher!

We can look at the leader being dressed in all white. White is often seen as pure and clean. However, in this dream not so much. In the book of 2 Corinthians, Chapter 11, Paul tells us that Satan himself masquerades as an angel of light. He goes on to say that it is not surprising that his servants masquerade as servants of righteousness.

To masquerade means to pretend to be someone one is not. To pose as someone or something else.

So, we see this convoy of men pretending to have the right to tell me what to do. We see this man in white pretending to be able to take what is not his. And then-we see us understanding that he has no right to even be on my porch or tell me what to do.

I see his shiny vehicle and his friends all sparkly in the sunshine leaving my driveway. Appearing to be great and fabulous, when in fact, they wanted to take me away from my family and take everything-everything else! All while looking good.

Let's take a moment and think about this.

What is stealing your joy?

What is coming in the back door of your life?

What is stealing our family? What is masquerading in our lives as something good and yet is harming us, and what can we do about it?

Pray. Seek God's word, and seek wise counsel if necessary! And wait expectantly for God to show up! Be bold, and speak God's word over your situation!

During the same week of this dream, I had a friend give me a surprise, a super cool soft grey t-shirt with "Fearless Isaiah 54:14" on the front. The giver, Pastor Bené Marsh, had not a clue about anything you have been reading.

BUT GOD DID!

The scripture on the shirt was perfect in timing for me.

Isaiah 54:14 reads,

"In righteousness, you will be established. Tyranny will be far from you; you will have nothing to fear. Terror will be far removed; it will not come near you."

Another beautiful reminder of what God was doing. He was teaching and he was reassuring, encouraging and right on time. And what a powerful scripture-which is a promise to us as we seek God.

As I press in to do the right things, to make right decisions, to have the right thoughts, God reaches back. In our dreams and when we are awake, we have nothing to fear! Terror will be removed and not allowed to come near us!

You can bet that Isaiah 54:14 became a new favorite scripture, and it is still committed to my memory. For me, this was another grand reminder of how God is ahead of us, how he wants to confirm what we are going through and what we are learning! Even when it is hard-He is with us!

More occurrences or encounters with evil spirits meant to frighten me still came. It was meant to rock my faith but this time it didn't. My belief in God's

control and protection was growing
stronger even though it was horrible to
be under attack.

However, my husband's faith had also
continued to grow over the years, and he
became increasingly unhappy that
something was in HIS home uninvited-our
home. Unhappy is really not the right
word; angry is definitely a better one.

This was new territory for me as Tommy
looked at it that way, but it was good
territory. I gained a new respect for him
as he prayed over our home. He blessed
all of the walls of our home with God's
word, and he prayed for me. And I
festered up a little bit of that angry,
too.

Tommy commanded authority, as head of our
household, over what was happening.
Silhouettes of coal-dark proportions
still moved around the room during the
night, and nightmares of horrific
proportions were still coming.

BUT something was different; I had a
distinct feeling it was about to be over!
Gosh, I was so ready. I was weary from
lack of sleep and tired of the same fear.

Still, I could feel the unity between
Tommy and I. United with God against this

situation, I was no longer crippling afraid when I saw or felt an evil presence or dreamed of something like it. My response, my ability to speak to the darkness, was getting faster and faster night after night.

Speaking to the presence, commanding it gone, it would leave. Whether I was asleep or awake, it worked. Learning to speak in God's authority, in the name of Jesus, worked every single time.

Most experiences were so similar to what I have already described that I won't bore you with them. I now understand with certainty Satan does not have any new tricks.

Think about that.

Think about what is coming against you today and yesterday and the day before that. As you think about that, remind yourself God's promises are the same every single day also, and God's promises are bigger than what is coming against you!
Isn't that awesome? The truth is absolutely that-awesome!

Learning this firmly, and reacting in it is absolutely freeing!

In the learning, I had another dream, another one that seemed to shake me to my core but in a good way.

In this dream, I step out of an elevator into a large dark area similar to a parking garage at night. Darkness and shadows are everywhere. Alone, I start walking to my left. I see movement from behind a block column to my right. I am startled, but I do not scream.

I can't. That same frozen muscle fear is keeping me from reacting...*again*.

My eyes are drawn to a large, tall, dark form. Reaching over six feet tall with a very wide shoulder spread, male in characteristics, looking very much like a man, yet it is not! It is not a human being. Void of all facial features and fuzzy all around its edges. The dark form seems made of fog and HATE. It is made of hate! I know that it hates me. I can feel it. I also know that it means me harm.

I can feel the anger; the presence of evil is so strong that I truly cannot explain it, but I feel it and taste it.

I can also feel its violence, terror, the very origin of it. I try to speak and cannot. Strangled with the force of what I see and feel! This. This Darkness! BUT THEN!

OH-BUT THEN, I start walking towards it!
TOWARDS IT! Towards the man yet not man!

Yes, towards it!

I am not frozen to my spot with fear as I
have been so very many times! I am moving
physically towards it! Walking in its
direction with the words "NO! NO! NO!"
coming loudly out of my mouth!

My words are slightly constricted but
they ARE coming out! My heart is
pounding! YET-I AM speaking against it
with the power of who I am as a child of
God! Commanding to be left alone by the
authority of Jesus Christ as I move in
its direction!

AND.IT.IS.WORKING!

I am becoming less afraid! I am
continuing to walk towards what has
frightened me for so long! I am
spiritually getting stronger with every
footstep, finally believing what God's
word says about Himself and me.

I AM who God says I am. I AM HIS. I AM
protected. Jesus has rule over this!
Jesus conquered all demons, darkness and
whatever else I don't know about on the
cross.

Feeling the certainty of God, "NO!" I say loudly. I, then, even louder still say- "I command you to leave me alone in Jesus' Name!" As I get within arm's reach of this evil spirit, I wake up from the dream. Unafraid!

UNAFRAID!

Wow!

I AM at peace!

Smiling, I lay in bed thankful for this dream! Thankful that I am not sweating with my heart racing! Thankful to not be upset by another nightmare that I am slow to win in or fighting for my life to breathe in. Thankful to be moving forward.

I knew with this dream I was a giant leap closer to conquering all fear, especially fear within the darkness of Satan and his foul helpers. God was walking me straight towards the defeat! With His protection I will not be harmed; I know I am learning to overcome whatever comes against me.

I trust this, and look for more of what God promises and find more assurance for us all-

God Himself-who is The God of peace will soon crush Satan under our feet and that the grace of our Lord Jesus will be with us (Romans 16:20).

AND

That the He, The Lord is faithful, and He will strengthen us and protect us from the evil one (2 Thessalonians 3:3).

Where is God wanting to lead you next?

What has He taught you already?

What does He still want you to learn?

Personal Notes

8- "Darkness Defeated"

The last instance was in my bathroom. There are some things that could be said about bathrooms. Symbolic stuff like: they are for cleaning things up and getting rid of waste.

That is kind of gross to think of, but yes. It fits.

Regardless, it was further away than in the past, and I knew what it was! I had just laid down when I felt something evil move into our room. That creepy feeling just washed right over me. I laid there a minute taking deep breaths and then sat up.

I saw a quick movement go into our bathroom. I jumped up and went in there. You're probably thinking I have lost my mind. Yes, maybe! Actually, my heart was beating a hole in my chest, and I did have some fear, but I truly wanted this to stop for good.

I also fully believed this could not touch me and that God was with me.

I had become well-acquainted with Ephesians 6:13-18. This is a powerful scripture about the armor of God, what protects us and how we are to fight our enemy. God's righteousness was before me, and I knew God's truth.

So shaky legs and all, just me and God's promises walk into our bathroom. I see in the corner a small area of darkness up against the wall. And yes, I said small, and I said up against the wall. It had filled the doorway as it entered, but as I walked into the bathroom with the light coming through our glass block window, I watched the darkness shrink. Partnered with God, dressed in His armor, trusting God's promises-this made it shrink!

The corner of my bathroom had been filled with this darkness, and now it kind of looked like a short cloud. But I knew its origin. It was the very presence of sickness, of anger, and of hate. I was very unhappy it was there; Tommy had taught me that. I had reason to be angry at it. I was sick of THIS!

As some light came in the room through the glass block window, I noticed the mirror in front of me and saw myself. I looked rough. Bad hair to be expected but my face looked weird like it was made of plastic.

What was this about? For a moment I stopped and stared, trying to move my face. Then I remembered I had other problems.

Focus! Isn't life always about focus?!

The enemy was trying to distract me, or perhaps I was trying to distract myself. I looked back to the corner and wanted to shout at this to get out and never come back! I felt again that I was choking out speech! And I was mad about that, too! I thought I was passed that! But again, it truly felt like hands were as tight as they could get on my throat! Satan clearly wanted to keep me from speaking God's word! He also definitely wanted to frighten me, distract me and keep me shut up!

This is the "grip of fear." It's having fear hold you way too tight.

I stood firm; I was not retreating. I slowly looked up to Heaven and managed a "In the name of Jesus, get out!" As my fear disappeared, so did the dark appearance of it. I looked back in the mirror. My face looked normal again, but I did still have the bad hair of course. I fell to my knees and started praying.

My first thought while praying was of restriction. Satan wants to restrict all of us. Seeing my face look unrealistic bothered me. I prayed for this, too!

"Please Father God, may I please never have a plastic looking face again in Jesus's precious name. May I be real inside and out, may I walk unrestricted and undistracted with you, God, all the days of my life, learning and believing your promises! THANK YOU, GOD, AMEN!"

On my way back to bed, I still remember smiling and thinking I should have prayed to sleep through a hurricane or spiritual battle like my husband can. For the "hundredth" time, I was up making all kinds of noise while he sleeps like a bear down for hibernation! "If I could focus on Jesus like Tommy focuses on sleep," I thought! Once again, I had been practically hollering as he slept the night away!

Actually, as crazy as it may sound, I would choose learning deep and wonderful things even through horrifying experiences over sleep. Because now the best story is next.

Close to two months later I had another dream. This dream seemed so real I hesitate to call it a dream. In reality, I was at war with the enemy in it and that still is as real as it gets.

Here is what I saw: I was in our bed and a dark figure, another one of those evil shadowy smoky looking fellows, came slinking into the room. I noticed it lingering by the door like so many times before. Sitting up quickly, I tried to scream at it to leave and could not. The same thing again and again! Ughh! Are you as sick of the same thing in this story? Are there things you are sick of in your own life?

Good news! We don't have to stay there!

So, the pitch-black darkness is there moving toward me, the grip of fear clutching my throat, strangling my vocal cords, hindering my speech.

OH, BUT THEN, but then I stopped. I stopped trying to command. I STOPPED trying to scream or even speak.

Remembering that as God's child I have the authority here, a flood of everything I knew God to be flooded my mind, and I simply looked straight at it and calmly shook my head side to side "NO."

Immediately the presence disappeared-vanished. Immediately! Gone with a head shake. Without any fight from me, I partnered with God- vanished with a "head shake." Did you get that??!!!

Can you just picture it? A calm, cool head shake "NO" ended the attack. Just wow! Like take a deep breath in and breathe out, and give a quiet "no" to what is coming against you-right now. God is so beautifully simple and beautifully powerful.

There was peace and lightness of heart like I have never felt in my life in my dream and as I came awake.

I awoke singing a praise song we had been singing recently at church. I was at such peace. More than I had ever known!

God's authority is that simple! I wanted to get up and jump up and down singing Hallelujah! God's authority is that bold and that soft! A simple head shake sent my fear packing!

Wow! I was on top of the world. Any claims Satan or fear had on me were and are finished. Renounced. Covered in the blood of Jesus! Finished! Hallelujah!

Why on earth had I been trying so hard? Just like the long hard lessons I had accepting God's grace, I had to learn long and hard lessons about God's authority and faith in his word!

I hope that you are not as hardheaded as myself! His word is true, all of it! We have the option to learn it, accept all of it, to walk in it and defeat the enemy!

It's not about me! Or You!

It is faith in action! Strength of God's word
in action!

"You, dear children, are from God and have overcome them, because the one who is in you is greater than the one who is in the world." 1 John 4:4.

Power is in learning! Learning how to dress for a fight, what my weapons were and how to use them. I had to trust in those weapons and the army I was fighting with! God's army!

The full armor of God (see Ephesians 6:13-18), not just part of it, all of it! Picture yourself as a solider getting ready for a battle!

We are taught in the Book of Ephesians to stand firm.
Meaning no retreating!

Because we are dressed!

Ready to fight!

Ready to win!

Let's put on our belt of truth and learn
what the Bible says about our battle.

While wearing our belt of truth-what
God's word actually says…LET'S STAY
FOCUSED! WHAT DOES THE BIBLE SAY?!

We are to put on our breastplate of
righteousness on our chest-protecting our
heart from harm based on who we are in
Christ!

YOU BELONG TO GOD!! CHRIST DIED FOR YOU!

We lace up our shoes fitted with the
gospel of peace. We are not the ones to
stir up strife! I AM CERTAIN THERE IS A
BIG ENOUGH DOSE OF STRIFE IN EACH DAY
WITHOUT ME BEING PART OF IT!

Our shield of faith is to be carried in
front of us. We hold it in front of us to
push forward and give us protection!
SOMEDAYS I HAVE TO IMAGINE THIS MORE LIKE
AN ARMORED VEHICLE-BUT STILL-IT IS TRUE!

Our salvation is described as putting on
a helmet. Being saved in Jesus, protects
our minds and our thoughts! WHEN FEARFUL
OR DISCOURAGED, ALWAYS RETURN TO WHOSE
YOU ARE! THIS WILL REMIND YOU OF WHERE HE
WANTS YOU-LIVING IN FREEDOM! LIVING IN
VICTORY!

Next, we have the sword of the Spirit.

If we are holding a sword to fight with, this scripture has us picturing the word of God, the promises of the Bible, as the sword!

IMAGINE SWINGING IT BACK AND FORTH, KILLING AND CUTTING DOWN WHAT IS COMING AGAINST YOU, YOUR FAMILIES, AND YOUR FRIENDS WITH THE STRENGTH OF WHO GOD IS AND WHAT GOD CAME TO GIVE US!

LIFE TO THE FULL!

Now, I do use a machete occasionally while hiking or hunting, and I am terrible at it. I don't just swing like a girl. I swing like a kid.

But you know what? That machete is made to hack down stuff, and regardless of my skill, it gets the job done!

Again, it is less about me and more about my weapon!

Thank The LORD!

A few weeks after this, I dreamed that I was in a field with lots of spring wildflowers and beautiful grass. A perfect sunny day outside, my favorite place to be. I see Jesus coming, walking through the field. Coming to me, coming to talk to me! I know exactly who He is.

He is dressed in white with shoulder-length dark hair. He looks at me as He draws closer. Such a sweet, sweet face. Bold, strong and kind at the same time. In this moment, Jesus spreads a gorgeous, shimmering, flowing piece of white fabric into the wind like you would shake out a blanket at the beach. The wind picked up the lightweight fabric. The sun's light was radiating off of it and through it.

I cannot explain the beauty of Jesus' face or the sweetness of the moment. I felt loved, accepted, and full of wholeness and joy.

Then, Jesus asked me, "Are you ready to get dressed for the wedding?" My heart beat picked up. My mouth went dry.

I actually said, "No."

I woke up immediately. Oh, how I grieved over this dream. I had thought I was ready. But I had said no!

I have grown a lot from that one. Searching for all the ways the Bible describes weddings, marriages, brides and grooms. Understanding the bride is the church as a whole. And as a whole, we aren't ready.

Until Jesus comes back to retrieve the church, his people, myself and everyone else who has received salvation must continue to press forward. Press forward in sharing with our friends, families and everyone God leads us to, who, God is to us.

Growing God's Kingdom, we are getting ready for the wedding-for Christ's return.

Praying, searching and reading more and more came after that dream. I want to be ready! I want to help God's church be ready! A couple of years have passed, and I am more ready than I was. I am more certain. That's a beautiful place to be. To be wrapped in the beautiful fabric of God's word. To be dressed for the wedding!

In the Book of Revelation, John, the writer, tells us of this beauty in verses 7-9 in Chapter 19.

It says, **"Hallelujah! For our Lord God Almighty reigns. Let us rejoice and be glad and give him glory! For the wedding of the Lamb (Jesus) has come, and His bride (God's people) has made herself ready. Fine linen, bright and clean,**

was given her to wear. Then the angel said to me, "Write this: Blessed are those who are invited to the wedding supper of the Lamb!" And he added, "These are the true words of God."

Some of us, like me, do not get to that place of certainty easily. But here is where the Spirit of Darkness gets defeated: in the certainty of Jesus, in the wedding, in the coming together with Christ to do HIS work. I praise HIM who is still completing what He started in me long ago.

Philippians 1:6 promises all of us that He will finish what he started. It is written-

"Being confident of this, that he who began a good work in you will carry it on to completion until the day of Christ." The day of Christ meaning when Christ returns.

Isn't that just awesome?

We can do what Ephesians 6 tells us to do! We can put on what protects us and let God fight for us! We can stand firm and not be harmed! We can have peace during a battle!

We all have to get dressed and stay dressed in what God's word promises us!

Focusing on God because he is right there with us in the war!

My thought process when God told me to write a book almost seven years ago was perhaps, I would understand why. Why me? Why would a child be tormented like that? Why would God allow it? What do I need to learn? What do I need to tell someone? I definitely did not expect to encounter the same as I wrote.

I may not have the completeness of the why figured out, but the pursuit has been amazing! Even in the fear, learning to stand strong in God's word and encourage others to do so will never leave me. Pursing the Bible for answers and strength cannot be taken from me or my household.

Learning that we overcome all kinds of bad "stuff" Satan throws our way by applying God's word and sharing our overcoming with others. This makes me happy to write.

The Holy Bible, which is God's letter to everyone, says in the Book of Revelation, "They overcame him (Satan) by the blood of the Lamb and by the word of their testimony."

We, as believers, are called to defeat Satan by the authority of Jesus Christ.

Jesus died for all our sins. He is the Lamb. He was the final sacrifice. That sacrifice joined us to our Heavenly Father, God.

Period.

As I have gotten to know God and His word, I have found promises of strength, promises of power and promises of who I am as God's daughter. I am loved, I am forgiven, and I have the power of God living inside of me through Jesus Christ.

This truth is what Satan wants to keep hidden from me and from you. He hides it in many ways. He represents his lies in different ways to different people. "For our struggle is not against flesh and blood, but against the rulers, against the spiritual forces of evil into the heavenly realms" (Ephesians 6:12).

What is the truth?

The answer is the same no matter what our struggle. God's word is the truth. But I had to learn what His word actually says and what it means. I then learned to apply it to my life and was willing to change.

Once we understand this, we become light. We become God's glory! We are God's glory when we stand on His truth. We are God's kingdom!

"For his IS the kingdom, and THE power, and THE glory forever."
(Matthew 6:13)

The word "*Glory*" actually means the manifestation of God's character, His ultimate power and moral perfection. When we accept this glory, it trumps the darkness. All darkness; the darkness of evil spirits, demons, nightmares and even negative thoughts and anxiety.

Our battle in overcoming Satan and his dark helpers is so much a part of who I am. It started very young, and I want others to understand Satan's tricks sooner than I did. I know that God wants you to understand it also! He told me so!

God longs for us all to know Jesus as our Savior, to know Him as our friend and for all of us to understand the power we have within us through Jesus! Power to overcome any struggle! To know that one little ray of light, the light of Jesus Christ, makes a dark area not dark anymore! I hope as you read this book with my stories, you see similar glimpses of God in your own life. I hope that you each own the battle that has been set before you!

Victory is in learning to partner with God Almighty!

"May we all learn to be strong and courageous in everything we do because the Lord our God goes with us wherever we go."

(Joshua 1:9)

I want to continue to encourage others to pray God's word. To learn what the Bible says! Now we have the internet to look up scripture on any topic, but I still like the dictionary, concordance and topical index in my Bible. You can look up what it says on a topic, whether it is fear or healing or grace or guilt.

What does the word of the Living God say? Use your Bible as a weapon. Use it as a tool to build your life, to build your house the way God would have it. His joy and His plan are better than any we could dream up for ourselves. I am so certain of this that I wish I could shout it from this page!

If we do this, God promises us peace! I want peace like I want food when I am hungry. Don't you?

"Peace I leave with you; my peace I give to you,"

John 14:27 promises.

Those beautiful words are straight from Jesus' mouth! Like water when I am thirsty!

Choose to be thirsty for God! Choose His peace!
Choose His power over the enemy, and choose to share your story!

In the Gospel of John after Jesus has risen from dead, he appears to his disciples, and twice he says the same thing.

" Peace be with you!!"

It even has the exclamation point at the end twice.

Jesus wanted them to know this was important.

As I study further, I look up the word peace. In English, peace is defined as freedom from disturbance; tranquility.

In Greek, it is the word Eirene, which means one, rest, and quietness.

In Hebrew, peace is translated to Shalom, which means harmony, wholeness, unity, and universal delight.

Universal Delight=Kingdom Peace.

The way God intended everything to be.

Peace=rest, wholeness, harmony, unity, tranquility and universal delight is with us through Jesus Christ.

Brings me right back to "His kingdom come-His will be done" as I pray for all things on my heart today.

May God's peace be with you and yours today!

His kingdom come-all of God's promises are with us!

The Lord's Prayer

Our Father, in Heaven,
hallowed by your name,
your kingdoms come,
your will be done
on earth as it is in heaven.
Give us today our daily bread.
Forgive us our debts,
as we also have forgiven our debtors.
And lead us not into temptation,
but deliver us from the evil one.
For yours is the kingdom,
and the power and the glory.
For ever and ever.
Amen.

Personal Notes

9- "Looking Ahead"

As the days come and go and seasons change, the beauty of the world around me continues to look different. I have had eyes to see some dark, ugly forces in my past, and I am looking forward to seeing the beauty of God's supernatural more and more in my future.

What we seek the Bible promises we find. Jesus waits at the door for us to let Him in, to share our lives with Him. This I want to see in my life and yours more and more. Each of us being equipped to do what Jesus did in others' lives-love, miracles, wisdom and deliverance.

I have gotten to "see" some amazing things already. Let me tell you some of my favorite experiences to date.

One evening while serving on our church's Prayer Team at a conference, a young woman came to me for prayer, and her breath was overwhelmingly horrid. I am a dental hygienist and am used to mouth odors, but this was the worst I had ever come in contact with.

I smelled raw, rotten, nasty sewage as the woman spoke.

She was beautiful. I had noticed her earlier because her hair was stunning and red, and she just stuck out to me. But as she spoke her prayer needs, I was having trouble focusing on her and her words. The smell as she spoke was so disgusting and so distracting.

My stomach was turning. My mouth was watering. *How could anyone's breath smell this bad?*

Forcing myself to listen, I asked God to help me help her and help me focus on what she was telling me. Immediately I heard the pain in her voice and saw the fear in her eyes as she told me her story. She had walked through a horrific attack of violence and rape. She spoke of fear being with her in everything she did and wanted to do because of what she had been through. And what she had been through was more difficult than I can imagine.

Tears fell hard down both our cheeks as I began to pray. Even while praying for her, I still smelled the garbage smell. It was in my nostrils and wouldn't get out. But I loved her regardless, praying for God to help her, and Holy Spirit was helping me.

Then, for the first time ever it crossed my mind that she might have some form of darkness attached to her. I felt led to pray for the spirit that had attached itself to her to be cast away.

I asked her to open her eyes and look at me. As she did, I asked the beautiful young woman if she wanted me to pray for any darkness to leave, and I asked if she felt she had something dark attached to her. With tears falling, she nodded "yes."

I spoke something simple like, "In the name of Jesus, foul spirit, I command you to leave."

Instantly, I smelled peppermint! It seemed as if I had a mouthful of it; it was in my nose, the coolness in my throat. Clean, crisp air filled my lungs.

I was in awe. Peppermint...Jesus smells like peppermint!

And foul spirits can evidently smell like sewage.

I should have recognized that I suppose. I will next time. I did not tell the young woman what all I had smelled. Maybe I should have, maybe not. She and I did take some time to discuss what she felt had been released from her and what God's word says.

We were both encouraged, excited and amazed!

I was thankful I had been through enough to have some wise counsel within me as well as understanding to share. And God definitely taught me something else new. He wants us to use all of our senses to feel, hear, see and smell his goodness and do His work! The Holy Spirit wants to partner with us in all of it!

God's presence is cool, refreshing, crisp and clean, filling each of us to the full with sweetness and goodness!

And now a story on HIS presence!

I had felt God pulling me towards noticing the posture in prayer. I love this as I do get on my knees to pray quite a bit but had felt led to do that even more so. Even during worship at church, I sometimes feel I should kneel, almost as if I long for it, yearn for it because I always find more closeness and refreshment from this position before God.

And who doesn't want more of that?

Amazingly, beautifully, God favored me with his touch during a moment of obedience to this call of submission. During an evening service at church, worship was flowing wonderfully. The symphony of believers were singing the praises of God loudly, and I suddenly had a strong desire to be on my knees in praise.

Now I am on a row with other people. I do not feel compelled to go to the front of the church and kneel. Nope, that would have been more common and so much easier. I feel as if I should somehow wiggle down right where I am and kneel at my chair. I actually sang through one song before being obedient. Questioning what I was feeling with the reality of the room full of other people.

Would they think I am crazy, weird, grieving, upset? Would I be a distraction? Was God really encouraging me to get on the floor right there at my chair where there was very little room? What if I just sat down and bent over?

I could go on and on with what was going on in my head. But I chose to just trust God and kneel down. To "just do it." I knew that the last thing the enemy would want me to do is kneel down before God my Father in private or in public. I knew the first voice or the inclination to kneel in praise was not the enemy.

It was God's.

On my knees, the fresh air of God moved over me, my lungs breathing deep the goodness of God in my life and the many things I had to be thankful for at the moment.

Singing the praise song with my face buried in my arms as they rested on my chair, knees on the concrete, time seemed to stand still. Then, I felt someone kneel down beside me. My hair moved, and I felt them brush my arm as their shoulder came against mine.

Tommy was on that side of me. Yet, my first thought was "Jesus, did you just kneel down with me?" I smiled so big at that as I enjoyed the surreal moment.

And then me being me, I had to look!

Opening my eyes, I somehow already knew that no visible person was kneeling beside me!

And there indeed was not anyone there that my eyes could see, but my spirit, soul and mind perceived it! I smiled and put my head back down and enjoyed the presence of being prayed with.

Letting my soul speak. I am so thankful for that moment. I look forward to more. Psalm 62:8 tells us, "Pour out our hearts to God; for He is our refuge."

In that moment, that's where I was, on my knees pouring my heart out, and God joined me. He bumped right up beside me, giving me permission to have an emotional, spirit-filled life and bring it all to him!

And if this isn't awesome enough, as I wrote this out, my friend Christy Bunch and I were sharing a conversation about some scripture and what God is inching us closer to in our lives.

And just then, she shares this scripture- "The Spirit of the LORD will rest on him-The Spirit of wisdom and of understanding, the Spirit of counsel and of power, the Spirit of knowledge of and of fear of the LORD-and he will delight in the fear of the LORD. *He will not judge by what he sees with his eyes, or decide by what he hears with his ears.*"

Just wow, more of what I was longing for!

This verse is found in Isaiah Chapter 11, verse 2 and 3. It is speaking of Jesus coming to earth, the foretelling of the Lord, Jesus arriving and how he was to be when He got here. And He was and is all of those things.

He was wisdom and knowledge, understanding, counsel and power. He did delight in the fear of the LORD, and he did not judge by his physical sight or physical hearing. He still is all of that with The Spirit of The LORD resting on Him, AND He left us to be all of those things also!

He left us to carry the torch and to continually fan the flames of the power of Heaven that He brought with Him until He returns!

"For we are God's workmanship, created in Christ Jesus to do good works, which God prepared in advance for us to do (Ephesians 2:13).

And now, using the words of Paul from the Book of Ephesians, I pray for each of you that are reading my testimony:

For this reason, I kneel before the Father, from whom his whole family in heaven and on earth derives its name. I pray out of the glorious riches he may strengthen you with power through his Spirit in your inner being, so that Christ may dwell in your hearts through faith. And I pray that you, being rooted and established in love, may have power, together with all the saints, to grasp how wide and long and high and deep is the love of Christ, and to know this love that surpasses

knowledge-that you may be filled to the measure of all the fullness of God.

Now to him who is able to do immeasurably more than all we ask or imagine, according to his power that is at work within us, to him be glory in the church and in Christ Jesus throughout all generations, for ever and ever, Amen!

Now-go look ahead with expectation of all God has you! For each of us! He makes all things new!
His mercies are new every morning! And all of His glory is yet to be seen, heard, felt or smelled!

I have learned not to allow myself the curiosity of things better left alone. I encourage everyone to leave books, movies or anything that might glorify Satan in any form, such as witches, sorcerers and the like, alone. God clearly forbids such things.

In the book of Acts, the town of Ephesus was a center for occult practices. Things did not go well for them until they renounced these practices. Renounce meaning, removed all ties to their occult practices. In the Book of **Deuteronomy**, God lets us know what He thinks about these things.

God speaking, it reads, **"Let no one be found among you who sacrifices his son or daughter in the fire, who practices divination or sorcery, interprets omens, engages in witchcraft, or cast spells, or who is a medium or spiritist or who consults the dead."**

God then tells them that anyone who does these things is detestable to the Lord! Personally, I want to be pleasing to the Lord! I will continually ask God to show me if I need to be doing something differently to abide in His peace, His shalom, His wholeness, unity, His rest.

Having confusing dreams and fearful confusing encounters has brought me to my knees. On my knees in God's sweet presence are the answers. I have renounced all of my previous behavior that opened the door to Satan and his helpers.

I declare this battle is over. Tommy has declared this is over. God's promises are beautiful, and they belong to all who choose to be part of His family! I look forward to understanding the dreams God does give me through the power of The Holy Spirit and growing in the next chapter of my journey!

The following verses reinforce my commitment to continued spiritual growth:

"Submit to God and we will have peace."
Job 22:21

I submit. I have peace.

"Align ourselves with our Heavenly Father and He will give us the desires of our heart."
Psalm 37:4

I focus on choices that please God. He blesses me.

"He anointed us, set his seal of ownership on us, and put his spirit in our hearts as a deposit, guaranteeing what is to come."
2 Corinthians 1:22

I have a purpose here on earth. I belong to God. He will return and take me to Heaven one day.

"Cast all our cares on him because He cares for us. Our enemy the devil prowls around looking for someone to devour. Resist Satan and he will have to flee from us!" 1 Peter 5:7

We are cared for by God. Satan wants to take us out of the game into a life of despair. God's truth sends Satan away from us!

I have learned that protection from our enemy Satan is not automatic even for believers. God's plan is to make us aware and even warn us. We must be alert, or we will not pick up on Satan's plans. He will try to take advantage of our nighttime and our daytime and of our families and friends.

Some doors are big and heavy; it can take two people or more to shut! In the Book of Matthew, Jesus tells us, "If two of you agree here on earth concerning anything you ask, My Father in heaven will do it for you." Jesus knew there would be times when we would need the help of others. I have learned to partner with other believers for that help when necessary.

<u>We must know our enemy!</u>

"For God is not a God of disorder but of peace." (1 Corinthians 14:33).

Even better Romans 8:31 tells us that if God is for us, who can be against us. Romans 13:14 tells us, "Rather clothe yourselves with the Lord Jesus Christ, and do not think about how to gratify the desires of the sinful nature."

Let's be thankful to shake our head "no" to what is not of God!

Hallelujah! That will always be my favorite part, the full authority of Christ, not me but Christ.

We will get more skilled at this as the days pass, and we continue to follow God's teaching, but it is there for us. Power to overcome and have peace within any situation that comes our way. It is there. Peace and power are waiting to partner with us!

I pray you each will be encouraged to stand firmly with God, and I really do hope that you learn more quickly than I did.

Although, what I have learned I do get to keep!

Let us all fix our eyes on Jesus!

With complete trust-all things are possible!

Including seeing the beautiful things of God, seeing what is moving in the supernatural for His glory. I look forward to getting to see more angels of light.

And a continuation of light over darkness.

A life where fear is silenced for good!

The Power of God's Armor and Army!

Ephesians 6:10-18

The Armor of God!

Get DRESSED!

Stay Dressed!

10 Finally, be strong in the Lord and in his mighty power. 11 Put on the full armor of God, so that you can take your stand against the devil's sceme. 12 For our struggle is not against flesh and blood, but against the rulers, against the authorities, against the powers of this dark world and against the spiritual forces of evil in the heavenly realms. 13 Therefore put on the full armor of God, so that when the day of evil comes, you may be able to stand your ground, and after you have done everything, to stand. 14 Stand firm then, with the **belt of truth** buckled around your waist, with the **breastplate of righteousness** in place, 15 and with your **feet fitted** with the readiness that comes from the gospel of peace. 16 In addition to all this, take

up the **shield of faith,** with which you can extinguish all the flaming arrows of the evil one. 17 Take the **helmet of salvation** and the **sword of the Spirit,** which is the word of God. 18 And **pray** in the Spirit on all occasions with all kinds of prayers and requests. With this in mind, be alert and always keep on praying for all the Lord's people.

Learning More About Our Armor

1) What is your belt of truth?
2) What is your breastplate of righteousness?
3) What does it mean to have your feet fitted with the gospel of peace?
4) What is your shield of faith?
5) What is your helmet of salvation?
6) What is your sword of the Spirit?
7) What does it mean to pray in the Spirit?

SCRIPTURE ON FEAR

So do not fear, for I am with you;
do not be dismayed, for I am your God.
I will strengthen you and help you;
I will uphold you with my righteous right hand.
Isaiah 41:10

For I am the LORD, your God, who takes hold of your
right hand and says to you, do not fear; I will help you.
Isaiah 41:13

I sought the LORD, and he answered me; he delivered
me from all my fears.
Psalm 34:4

The angel of the LORD encamps around those who fear
him, and he delivers them.
Psalm 34:7

Be strong and courageous. Do not be terrified because of
them, for the LORD your God goes with you; he will
never leave you nor forsake you.
Deuteronomy 31:6

When I am afraid,
I will trust in you.
In God, whose word I praise,
in God I trust; I will not be afraid.
what can mortal man do to me?
Psalm 56:3-4

For God did not give us a spirit of timidity, but a spirit
of power, of love and of self-discipline.
2 Timothy 1:7

Even though I walk
through the valley of the shadow of death,
I will fear no evil,
for you are with me;
your rod and your staff,
they comfort me.
Psalm 23:4

Have I not commanded you? Be strong and courageous. Do not be terrified; do not be discouraged, for the LORD your God will be with you wherever you go.
Joshua 1:6

The LORD is my light
and my salvation-
who shall
I fear?
The LORD is
the stronghold
of my life-
of whom
shall
I
be
afraid?

Psalm 27:1

Made in the USA
Columbia, SC
26 August 2019